The Development of Sustainable Tourism

Lars Aronsson

CONTINUUM
London and New York

Continuum

Wellington House, 125 Strand, London WC2R 0BB

370 Lexington Avenue, New York, NY 10017-6550

First published 2000

British Library Cataloguing-in-Publication Data

A catalogue record for this book is available from the British Library.

ISBN   0 8264 4884 4 (hb)
                0 8264 4885 2 (pb)

Typeset by Ben Cracknell Studios

Printed and bound in Great Britain by Bath Press

Contents

CONTENTS

Part 2: Lifestyle During Leisure

Part 3: Tourism and Leisure Travel

CONTENTS

Part 4: The Destination

Part 5: Conclusions
Sustainable Tourism and Mobile Leisure Development: What Lessons Can Be Learnt?

Figures

Tables

Acknowledgements

The Development of Sustainable Tourism is built on 'Sustainable Development of Tourism?', which is the final report from the project 'Sustainable Tourism Development'. The project extended over a relatively long period, from 1992 until its completion in June 1997. The book is also the result of further research after the completion date. The project was jointly funded by a number of Swedish authorities: Forskningsrådsnämnden (Council for Planning and Coordination of Research), Statens råd för byggnadsforskning (Council for Building Research) and Länsstyrelsen i Värmland (The County Administration in Värmland). Karlstad University also provided funding. I would like to express my appreciation to all these institutions. The work has been both instructive and demanding and it has been extremely interesting and stimulating to examine questions relating to sustainable development and the environment despite the fact that the concept of sustainable development in particular has not been easy to grasp.

Many colleagues have made valuable contributions during the course of the project and I am grateful to them all. My special thanks go to those who acted as a reference group for the project: Brynjulf Alver, University of Bergen, Lennart Bäck, Uppsala University and Sondre Svalastog, University College of Lillehammer; to those who worked together with me on various aspects of sustainable tourism and leisure: Lage Wahlström, Bertil Vilhelmson and Lotta Frändberg, Göteborg University, Klas Sandell, Örebro University, David Crouch, Anglia University and Norman McIntyre, Griffith University. Berit K. Svanqvist and Elisabeth Brandin of Karlstad University were engaged in the project for a period. Göran Hoppe, Uppsala University, Reinhold Castensson, Linköping University, Klas Sandell and Sondre Svalastog have read the project report and have provided many helpful comments and suggestions for improvements. I am appreciative of all the support I have

ACKNOWLEDGEMENTS

received from colleagues in the Department of Geography and Tourism and in the Research Unit for Tourism and Leisure at Karlstad University. Many thanks to Michael Cooper, Karlstad University, who has translated the Swedish text into English. The picture on the front cover of the book was taken by the photographer Ove Johnsson at midsummer and it represents timber rafts (an ecotourism product) on the Klara River in the province of Värmland in Sweden. Last, but not least, I would like to thank my family for putting up with a husband and father who sometimes was somewhere else in his thoughts than at home, and my gratitude to my parents (my father died suddenly during the course of the work) who in various ways have given me the opportunity to work in a very privileged profession. Finally, please note that the views expressed are mine alone and that I am entirely responsible for any inconsistencies and mistakes.

LARS ARONSSON
Karlstad 1999

Introduction

THE APPROACH ADOPTED

This book attempts to present a somewhat different approach to that which is generally found in the literature on the development of sustainable tourism and mobile leisure activities. One example of a recurring theme in the text is the adoption of a time–space aspect on sustainability and tourism, which is primarily derived from time-geography.

After Part I, which deals with general aspects and international examples of sustainable tourism development, the book is based on the tourist's journey or, put in other terms, the various components of the tourism system. This means that Part II deals with the conditions for tourist and leisure activities; it is based, in particular, on the concept of lifestyle. Part III deals with tourist travel itself in the modern and late modern 'highly mobile' society. Both Part II and Part III focus on the problems caused by high and low mobility and the impact of travel on the environment. The perspective is in one sense the idea of a global environment, global resources and solidarity. Part IV considers the destination. Apart from physical adaptation to the environment, this Part also considers the other consequences of tourism in a place or, in other words, questions of economic, social and cultural sustainability. In this Part a case-study is used to show how regional social planning can also include sustainable tourism development. Furthermore, the perspective is more oriented towards the local and towards production theory than in the earlier parts. Finally, Part V considers the lessons that have emerged from the material. The approach I have adopted means that sustainability and environmental issues in the three components of the tourism system are considered in some detail and, at the same time, they are related to society in general. I have thus attempted to achieve a holistic perspective on the factors that affect the sustainability of tourism.

There is a general discussion in the book on sustainability and environmental issues which can be applied to the majority of countries in the rich world. The rich empirical material with both qualitative and quantitative data and the practical examples are based on material which primarily relates to Swedish conditions, but there are examples from other countries. Sweden is among the leading nations of the world when it comes to environmental issues and in adapting activities to the environment, which would suggest that other countries might be interested in developments in Sweden.

I am by profession a human geographer and the text is clearly influenced by some of the central concepts in the discipline. What I believe that human geography can contribute to research fields such as tourism studies, cultural studies and environmental studies is theoretical reasoning and empirical material on key concepts such as processes in time–space, places, lifestyles linked to landscape and environment. These key concepts permeate the book. The purpose of this introduction is first of all to set the text in the larger context of the various subsystems in modern society and its organization, and a number of central processes which exert a strong influence on the development of society and tourism. Second, the concepts of sustainability and tourism, and environmental issues are placed in a more general research framework. I have no ambition to provide a comprehensive introduction; it should be seen as a rough sketch, which all readers can supplement and compare with their own map.

GENERAL COMMENTS ON THE VIEW OF SOCIETY

There have always been changes and processes in nature. However, through his activities, during the last two hundred years in particular, people have had an unprecedented impact on nature. The intensity and extent of various environmental problems have increased dramatically. This is primarily a result of how we organize society, where the way the economic system has functioned during the industrial age has led to excessive exploitation of raw materials, poorly developed waste management, and so forth. The political, social and cultural systems have, in many cases, gone hand in hand with the economic system and this is a strong contributory factor to the present 'unsustainable' approach to nature (and also to local cultures) and to the environmental problems we are facing. The problems manifest themselves in different ways in different places in the world. At the same time, the social system and lifestyles of the rich world are spreading rapidly to most corners of the globe. Tourism is part of this development and I shall comment briefly on this.

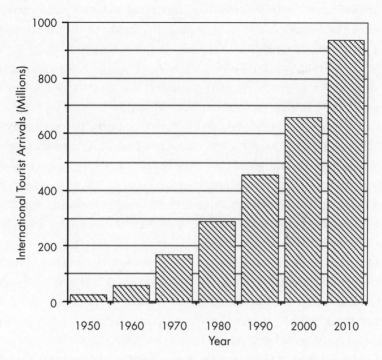

Figure 1. Development, trends and prospects of international tourist arrivals (millions), 1950–2010.
Source: World Tourism Organization (1992, 1994a, 1994b, 1995)

As is implicit in Figure 1, the number of international tourist arrivals has increased by over 2000 per cent from 1950 to 1994. In 1950 there were 25 million journeys crossing national borders. The figure for 1994 was 528 million. The internal tourist traffic within countries is estimated to be ten times as extensive. According to the estimates of the World Tourism Organization (WTO) the number of international tourist arrivals will be over 650 million in the year 2000 and over 900 million in 2010. The annual growth rate up to 2010 will be between 3.5% and 4.5% according to WTO (Burns and Holden 1995, pp. 2–4; Williams, S. 1998, p. 47). Furthermore, the tourist industry employs more than 130 million people worldwide and makes annual capital investments in excess of US$ 400 billion (Finnish Tourist Board 1993).

It is clear that tourist travel has become a primary consumer good linked with the lifestyle of modern and late modern society. What has created this powerful development and what social processes are connected with it? The dramatic increase in tourist travel is partly dependent on such factors as: increased material standards, the development of the infrastructure and means of transport and the fact that people have more leisure. It is this type of factor that provides the conditions for the increase in travel, which is mainly to be found among the population of the rich world. My argument in this introduction is that the development of tourism is linked with a number of overarching social processes. Together, these form major parts of the context for tourism (cf. Aronsson and Wahlström 1999, pp. 63–77).

My point of departure is that the driving force or motor behind today's global developments is primarily the economic system, which in its turn is closely linked to the political sphere. Examples of collective economic actors with a major impact on developments are the worldwide financial markets and transnational companies. The political system affects developments through, for instance, the regionalization of the world in organizations such as the European Union and the North American and Southeast Asian trade agreements.

The first process I shall deal briefly with and relate to tourism is globalization. The process of globalization is complex and is made up of a number of components. Apart from the driving forces mentioned above, it also consists of forces of social and cultural change, which are based, among other things, on the development and impact of information technology and mass media. These processes have an impact on people's everyday lives and this means that it is in this context that the processes become visible. The process of globalization consists in part of an increase in the extent and intensity of worldwide communications, time–space compression, converging lifestyles and migration (Harvey 1989, 1996; Massey and Jess 1995; Törnqvist 1998). Globalization may be said to be a process where relatively separate places on earth have come to interact and are thereby seen as a single conceptual space. Individual places are a unique combination of local characteristics and global processes. These processes change the conditions and structures of the places economically, socially, culturally and ecologically. In its turn, this means that the identity and distinctive character of the socially and culturally constructed places is changed over time. In a physical sense, places can be seen as 'bound' points in the great whole that is termed space. In modern society space is often considered to be compressed as a result of the development of communication systems (infrastructure for traffic, information technology and the media). On the other hand, the social and economic networks have a tendency to become increasingly extended in space. Further, a place is populated by various categories of people, e.g. as regards class, life modes and lifestyles, who in their turn have different positions of power. The actors in a place are linked together and are dependent on each other through social and economic relations in space. With this approach, a place is mainly seen as a meeting place where the actors' trajectories are linked together in time–space or activity space. Activity space may be anything from local to global in character depending on the activity (Hägerstrand 1989; Massey and Jess 1995). As is apparent, the processes affect places and people's everyday lives, and we are becoming increasingly dependent on the overarching systems. These developments are also linked with the new individualism. The rich countries in the world, and in particular the Western ones, have become increasingly multicultural and the people more lifestyle-oriented.

These arguments relate to tourism in several ways. First, tourism in itself can be seen as a system of links and nodes (places), e.g. the journey from home to the destination and back again. In modern society there have been major changes in activity space – greater complexity and greater spatial diffusion. Travel in connection with tourism and leisure activities is an example of this. Globalization presupposes a highly mobile society and this in itself causes many environmental problems. Second, tourism is part of the exchange between places, an exchange which consists of many parts. Apart from the effects of mobility, tourism produces an impact on a place and thus contributes to the continuous process of change. Tourism forms part of many lifestyles and is a form of globalization, and it is at least superficially seen as a mass phenomenon and contributes to the mixed, multicultural society.

A further central development process in modern society, which is interwoven with the process of globalization, is the spread of the consumer culture (or commodification). The commodification of places and cultures leads to problems in the meeting of cultures, which would seem to be of increasing importance in a multicultural society. The trend is very clear in tourism where experiences and places are commodified and linked with demand (Bell and Valentine 1997; Lury 1996; Rojek 1998; Urry 1990), as Hughes says: 'In modern tourism Western capitalism appears to have developed the ultimate consumer' (Hughes 1998, p. 23).

From the viewpoint of the tourist, tourism is based on symbolic value. For the tourist it is a world of sensations and experiences. For the person who markets and sells tourism experiences it is a matter of exchange value. The symbolic value has become a 'tourism product'. In this case it is a question of commodifying experiences and places to achieve an economic exchange. Thus the seller markets and sells by means of myths and symbols (Blom 1994; Crang 1998; Morgan and Pritchard 1998; Selwyn 1996; Urry 1995; Wahlström 1984).

For the resident population in a place the place's resources may also be said to be a matter of utility value alongside the other values. In some cases it is a question of a conflict between the place being a living space for the residents and being commodified and adapted to temporary visitors. It may be said that certain forms of tourism entail the exploitation and 'packaging' of parts of the local culture and nature in order to sell them as an experience. On many occasions the original purpose of a phenomenon in the local culture is adapted to make it saleable. Much of the current literature on tourism is very critical of the commodification of phenomena for tourist purposes (e.g. that commodification contributes to cultural change) and it is justified in this. At the same time, we live in a world where products of many kinds are based on the commodification of something – there is not really any alternative to the capitalist system today. One may ask whether it is wrong to invest in tourism as an industry in a place which is in decline if it is thereby possible to reverse the economic trend. It is perhaps more a question of how tourism is developed and represented. What determines whether tourism is good or bad for a place (and thus for its sustainability) is both the type and extent of its impact and the context, the structure and the processes of which tourism forms part.

Another condition that is typical of modern society is the functional division of space. Housing, workplaces, service, education and leisure activities are spatially widely separated in many places, which also contributes to high mobility and places demands on a well-developed infrastructure with rapid and often long-distance transport of goods and people. The spatial division of functions can be seen as a material effect of modernization and is coupled both to the process of urbanization and to the specialized division of labour in society. Altogether, this type of development creates significant environmental problems, in the form, for instance, of extensive travel.

The above reasoning implies changeable places and landscapes and a different or new perception of space, among other things through the compression of time–space. Industrialism's landscape can be designated a production landscape with factories and other infrastructure for production. The late modern landscape consists, to a much greater extent, of symbols (signifiers) of the consumer society in the form of service establishments such as restaurants, cafeterias and petrol stations. The earlier, more unambiguous production landscape has thus become a mixed landscape – both for experiences, and visual production and consumption at the same time (Crang 1998; Ringer 1998; Wahlström 1997). The present leisure landscape consists of everything from simple walking and cycling trials, training tracks and facilities in the proximity of built-up areas to a network of transport systems, accommodation, service and activity facilities for tourism at a distance.

The purpose of this outline description of some of the central processes in modern society has been to provide a framework for a discussion of the issues concerning the sustainable development of tourism and leisure activities. We shall return explicitly to some of the key concepts whilst others are implicit in the following discussion.

ADAPTING TOURISM TO THE ENVIRONMENT

Adapting industries to the environment has become increasingly important in modern society, particularly in the rich world. There are two reasons for this. Apart from the fact that environmental adaptation has become a means of economic competition, environmental ethical values, concerned with preserving the physical environment or maintaining it at a reasonable level, are growing in importance. A common approach in tourism research is to see the environmental aspects as an effect of tourism production. Tourism's production process is a complex phenomenon with companies in a large number of different sectors. The various sectors in tourism are faced with different types of environmental problems. Further, there is a multitude of organizations and authorities that influence the development of tourism. All parts of the production and consumer process have an environmental aspect and it is not least important in connection with the choice of journey and behavioural patterns during the journey. Therefore it is vital to provide the consumer with environmental information. As I have suggested, it is possible to see tourism's environmental problems from both a macro and a micro perspective. From the macro perspective, tourism's negative environmental impact may largely be seen as a consequence of the short-sighted policy of commodifying nature and culture for tourist purposes (Karlsson 1994). An overarching question is whether it is possible to bridge the conflict between economic profitability and adaptation to the environment – to create an economically and environmentally sustainable production. Environmental problems generally require regulations alongside changes in lifestyle, and the solutions are dependent on acceptance by the economic system. A partnership is probably required between the government, industry, the green movement and science in order to reconstruct the capitalist economy in a direction which is more adapted to the environment. From the micro perspective, previous studies show that it is difficult to adapt tourist journeys to the environment even though we normally have an eco-friendly attitude at home (Frändberg 1993, pp. 9–35). The difficulties lie in the fact that positive environmental behaviour when travelling is practically complicated, or perhaps we find it convenient also to take a vacation from our environmental responsibility when we are tourists.

SOME APPROACHES IN TOURISM RESEARCH

The following is a general and relatively comprehensive definition of tourism studies: Tourism comprises people's journeys to places other than those where they live and work, and the activities carried out during the journey and at the destination. Tourist journeys can be both for leisure and work, e.g. participating in conferences. The tourist industry, in its turn, includes all the businesses which in various ways provide service for the tourists. Tourism studies is thus the study of people and their mobility, people's activities at the non-everyday place and the context for tourism. As regards tourism's production processes, tourism studies considers the conditions and resources for tourism, the various parts of the production process, how images of places and products are created and conveyed as well as distribution in general, consumption of and demand for tourism, and the various impacts which occur in a place (economic, social and cultural, physical, geographic and ecological). Tourism studies also include the tourist's social background, motives and expectations and what happens at the places visited, e.g. development and planning issues and the encounter with the local culture and the local residents (cf. Mathieson and Wall 1982, p. 1).

Tourism is, like the majority of societal phenomena, of a multi-disciplinary nature, where research may be pursued from a number of different angles. Tourism research has so far been mainly in an empirical and inductive phase. Basic knowledge of this worldwide, socially and economically significant phenomenon has so far been gathered primarily through a large number of case-studies. Today it is possible to discern some form of theory on tourism produced by scholars in human geography, sociology and anthropology and the research fields of tourism studies and cultural studies (cf. Butler and Pearce 1995; Ringer 1998; Rojek and Urry 1997; Selwyn 1996; Smith and Eadington 1992; Urry 1990, 1995).

It is an enormously demanding and difficult task to attempt to describe the current research situation on tourism issues. A large number of scientific articles are being published in journals and presented at conferences. There has been extensive publication of books in English on tourism in recent years. However, I shall provide some (very generalized) information about research relating to my perspective on sustainable tourism development.

One way of classifying research on tourism is to start with the metaphor mentioned above: 'the tourist's journey' (Aronsson 1993; Frändberg 1998). This leads to a tripartite classification:

1. Background factors for the journey, e.g. lifestyle and life mode and other conditions for and restrictions on travel.
2. The journey itself where it is classified as tourist travel.
3. The conditions for tourism at the destination and its impacts.

Given this classification, the predominant aspect of research on tourism during the last 25 years in the Anglo-Saxon sphere would seem to be research on the destination (cf. de Kadt 1976; Gunn 1988; Lanfant *et al.* 1995; Lockhart and Drakakis-

Smith 1997; Mathieson and Wall 1982; Murphy 1985; Pearce, D. 1981, 1987; Ringer 1998; Selwyn 1996; Smith and Eadington 1992).[1] What would seem to be the next most common area of research concerns various types of background factors in the tourist, including lifestyle and demand. Here sociologists and anthropologists have concentrated on making typological classifications of tourists. Some of these classifications relate to the demands for resources from different groups of tourists (cf. Cohen 1972; Karlsson 1998; Karlsson and Lönnbring 1998; Lowyck *et al.* 1992; Smith, V. L. 1989; Svalastog 1994). Further, economists have concentrated on the segmentation of tourists from a marketing standpoint. In general terms, the following quotation provides an insight into the status of research on typologies.

> As in other fields of tourism, the typology literature is fragmented, lacks cohesion, and is without much sense of common purpose and central direction. A major reason for this is the multifaceted nature of tourism which makes any comprehensive analysis or classification very difficult, and consequently has led researchers to concentrate on certain aspects (e.g. demand, development, or impact), to focus on particular types of tourism (e.g. coastal or alpine), or to limit themselves to selected areas. (Pearce, D. 1992, p. 21)

Finally, what would seem to be the least researched area is the journey itself. It should be pointed out that this field has been relatively extensively researched by transport researchers, however, without any particular focus on tourist journeys (cf. de Paauw and Perrels 1994; Frändberg 1996, 1998; Krantz and Vilhelmson 1996; Müller 1992; Vilhelmson 1988, 1990, 1994b; Whitelegg 1993). Even research on the environmental impact of tourism seems to follow the same pattern. The most extensive research would seem to be on the various types of impact tourism has at the destination. This includes studies on the wear and tear effect of tourism, littering, conflicts concerning the use of land, planning and management methods to solve these problems. Further, during the 1990s there has been a whole range of titles mainly on such areas as sustainable tourism and ecotourism. Studies of sustainable tourism are generally structural and concern the macro level (Hägerhäll 1988; Hunter 1995; Travis 1992). Studies of ecotourism are often limited to the analysis and evaluation of special projects (Hanneberg 1996; Place 1991; Weaver 1991; Wilkinson 1989). Naturally, there are other ways of classifying research on sustainable tourism than the three I have referred to. Other topics in research on the consequences of tourism relate to mass tourism versus small-scale tourism and tourism in poor versus rich countries (Smith and Eadington 1992). Squire (1998, pp. 81–2) and Williams, S. (1998, pp. 5–18) provide an overview of the various directions in research on tourism-geography and tourism. There are also a number of books and articles which have considered the question of sustainable tourism from a holistic perspective, e.g. Burns and Holden (1995) and

Hunter (1995). What in particular distinguishes this book from those just mentioned is the time-geographic perspective with the emphasis on processes in time–space. In recent years the traditions in cultural studies seem to have rubbed off on tourism research and revitalized it as regards holistic perspective, problemization and theory generation.

PART 1

Sustainable Tourism Development

CHAPTER 1

Society, Tourism and the Environment

INTRODUCTION

Today people in the rich world live in a consumer culture where they can almost endlessly satisfy their material needs with new products, but where also certain immaterial needs can be more than satisfied by, for instance, travel. It has gradually become clear that this lifestyle involves a considerable waste of resources and has a number of negative effects on the environment. In the foreword to 'The State of the World, 1996' the Worldwatch Institute states that global development is moving at an extremely rapid pace and that, among other things, the enormous growth in population since the 1950s and the consumer culture with a 400 per cent increase in world trade since the 1950s are having a crucial impact on global ecology.

> How long can this process continue within a limited space? The ecological impact of this growth can already be clearly seen globally . . . At present the state of the world is a matter of some concern; at the same time the opportunities for positive action have perhaps never been greater. (Worldwatch Institute 1996, pp. 7–8, my translation)

In recent years the eco-labelling of goods has become increasingly common in much of the rich world. This tendency is even noticeable in the area of tourism and leisure; there are, for instance, environmental criteria for hotels and travel. The question is whether a greater use of environmentally 'better goods and services' is sufficient. Perhaps we shall have to change our whole lifestyle and consume less resources in order to achieve what might really be termed more sustainable development. If people, in the rich world in particular, can make a radical change to a more eco-friendly lifestyle, this in its turn may lead to major changes in production and consumption. At the same time, we must formulate criteria and change our decisions and rules if we are to achieve a structural shift towards more sustainable development in both an international and national perspective.

The travel and tourism industry is currently one of the largest industries in the world together with the oil industry and building and construction. Even in Sweden the tourism industry is becoming increasingly significant. Measured in terms of Gross Domestic Product (GDP), it is larger than agriculture, forestry (excluding the processing industry) and fishing together. On behalf of Turistdelegationen[2] (the Swedish Tourist Delegation), Statistiska Centralbyrån (Statistics Sweden) estimated the turnover from tourism in 1995 at about 116 billion Swedish crowns (SEK), which is about 3.2 per cent of the nation's GDP. Furthermore, it was estimated that about 132,500 people were employed full-time in tourism in Sweden in some form or other.[3] This figure represents about 3.5 per cent of the total number employed in the country. In many regions tourism grew in importance throughout the 1980s. However, there was some stagnation and decline in the early 1990s, partly because of the general recession. Starting with the winter season in 1992–93, the tourism industry has, however, begun to recover. This positive development, which was partly a result of the devaluation of the Swedish crown, has continued up to the present. During the first half of the 1990s tourism has undergone structural changes. Sweden attracted more foreign visitors than before whilst Swedes travelled abroad less than they did in the 1980s. The Swedish regions with the largest number of visitors and the greatest economic effects from tourism are the metropolitan areas, Stockholm, Göteborg and Malmö, the coastal areas including the islands, and the mountains.

At the same time as tourism is becoming increasingly important in economic terms, it is also having both positive and negative impacts in countries and regions (cf. Aronsson 1989, 1993, 1997; Commonwealth Department of Tourism 1994, pp. 19–22; Gunn 1988; Krippendorf 1989; Lea 1988; Mathieson and Wall 1982; Murphy 1985; Pearce, D. 1981; Pearce, P. L. 1988). Some of the more important positive economic aspects mentioned in the literature include greater income for both private companies and the public sector, and more jobs. Negative economic aspects include high costs for parts of the public sector, short-term exploitation of resources for quick profits and the problem of the seasonal nature of tourism. Among the positive environmental consequences of tourism are that it can stimulate the preservation of natural and cultural areas and contribute financial resources to the preservation and administration of the environment. Its negative environmental consequences are often said to be encroachment on natural and cultural environments, geographical and physical change and ecological damage as well as pollution and litter.

In general, tourism entails interaction with the local community, which may lead to change. The positive aspects of tourism from a social and cultural perspective are that it can create the economic conditions for establishing new activities and providing social services and that it can lead to the preservation of cultural values and traditions. Its social and cultural disadvantages are that it may produce a sense of overcrowding between residents and tourists, competition and conflict over local assets, e.g. areas of natural beauty and culturally interesting sites and that the local culture may become commercialized and thus lose its original value. Tourism often has a cumulative impact, which means that it is better to solve the problems caused by tourism where they occur rather than move the activities and exploit new untouched resources.

In recent years increasing attention has been given to the negative effects of tourism, in particular its environmental impact. Apart from environmental criteria, programmes and action plans have been developed for sustainable tourism development for regions, countries and for tourism industries in countries such as Australia, Canada, Finland and Sweden. Even influential non-governmental organizations have produced criteria and action plans for sustainable tourism and ecotourism. These include the World Tourism Organization, the World Wide Fund for Nature (in the US and Canada, World Wildlife Fund) and the Ecotourism Society.

THE IMPORT OF THE TERMS 'SUSTAINABLE TOURISM' AND 'SUSTAINABLE LEISURE ACTIVITIES'

Studying sustainable development is associated with certain difficulties. The term is normative and there is a clear subjective ambition in sustainable development. The term is also relative. There is no absolute sustainable development, rather sustainability can be seen as a process towards something which, from some angles, is more sustainable than what has been before. Further, the concept is multi-dimensional, which makes it difficult to define. If it is interpreted in its broadest sense, it has economic, social and cultural, political, geographical and ecological aspects, which means that we must adopt an interdisciplinary approach. The economic aspect is primarily a matter of satisfying human material needs and goals. The social and political aspects relate in general to questions of equality, justice and influence, whereas the geographical ones concern, for instance, the consequences of man's spatial behaviour and the ecological ones the problem of protecting the natural variety and preserving the natural cycle intact. A further point is that:

the sustainability concept is a contextual one, i.e. there is a need for specifications until it becomes practicable. The simplest aspects of such specifications answer questions like: sustainable – at which level and at which time perspective; sustainable – for whom; sustainable – with regard to which system and with regard to which function. (Svedin 1992, p. 296)

As its content is broad, the concept provides an important holistic perspective on society and environmental issues. However, to define and delimit the term for research purposes is much more difficult. A frequently used definition is the one found in the Brundtland Commission's report *Our Common Future*: 'to ensure that development provides for today's needs without jeopardizing the chances for coming generations to satisfy their needs' (Hägerhäll 1988, p. 22, my translation). Later in the same text we find the following comment:

In the final analysis, however, sustainable development is not a fixed state of equilibrium but rather a process undergoing continual change in which the use of resources, the type of investment, the direction of technological development, and institutional change are in harmony with both today's needs and those of tomorrow. (Hägerhäll 1988, p. 23, my translation)

The quotation stresses the need for social, institutional and structural change if we are to achieve a more sustainable world. I may add that greater sustainability is also a matter of adjusting our lifestyle, values and cultural concepts. Furthermore, like all other living creatures and matter, we human beings are parts of ecosystems which are continually interacting and changing together (Leimgrüber and Imhof 1998, p. 3).

Tourism and leisure activities are also a complex area, which means that any study of the field generally has to be limited to certain aspects. The import and effects of tourism and leisure travel differ from situation to situation, and this means that the consequences of developing more sustainable forms will be considerable. Like the concept of sustainable development, tourism and leisure can be considered from various angles, as is exemplified by the following points.

- Lifestyle factors affect the choice and content of tourism and leisure travel. Leisure travel can also be seen as a way of manifesting a special lifestyle (Veblen 1976). If we are to achieve long-term sustainable development, it is essential that we as individuals change our attitudes, behavioural and consumer patterns. Explaining the role people play in the consumer society and its negative impact on the environment is partly an educational task.
- Tourism and leisure travel involve movements in space by people and these, depending on the means of transport they choose, have varying effects on the environment. From the standpoint of sustainability this means that we should, for instance, use more eco-friendly means of transport than aircraft and cars,

develop technology which will enable us to adapt existing forms of transport to the environment, make long-term infrastructural changes in the transport system, and channel leisure activities to the local environment thus reducing the need for transport.

- Tourism and leisure travel entail the spatial movement of materials. These might be building materials for constructing facilities for tourism and leisure activities, or provisions for consumption. This has an impact both on the environment as a result of the transportation involved and on the level of the local multiplier effects in the economy. Local economies can be made more sustainable in connection with the development of tourism and leisure facilities by increasing the level of local procurement and the use of local labour.

- Tourism and leisure travel entail economic transactions which have spatial implications. Tourism is often seen as a service which is both produced and consumed at the same time and in the same place. However, tourism produces a flow of money which, from the standpoint of the local community, for instance, has material significance as a result of its effect on the structure of industry and commerce and its possible economic utility for the local residents. In countries like those in Europe the tourism industry may enable rural areas, which often have few commercial alternatives, to become more diverse in their commercial structure and therewith more economically viable. Thus an area should not rely on just one commercial alternative.

- The human movements in space which tourism and leisure travel entail have place-specific consequences in the form of encounters between people, which may lead to social contacts and the transfer of culture or to conflict. From the viewpoint of sustainability it is important which form of tourism evolves and how it interacts with the local community. Further, the extent of tourism and its temporal variations are often crucial for the results of the encounters between visitors and hosts (Aronsson 1993, 1997).

- The development of tourism has consequences for physical planning, as regards, for example, the use of land resources, and leads to local political decisions regarding exploitation for tourist activities. Sustainable tourism development underlines the importance of ensuring the decisions and measures are accepted locally.

- Human movements in tourism and leisure travel have geographical and ecological consequences, in connection both with exploitation for tourist and leisure facilities and with the activities as such, for instance wear and tear, and litter. It is vital that new tourist and leisure facilities are adapted to the local community through, for instance, planning and management measures.

As we have shown, sustainable tourism and sustainable leisure activities can be

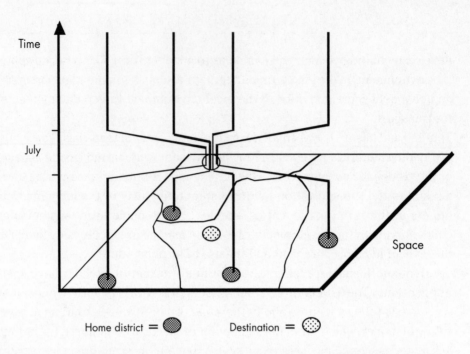

Figure 1.1. An illustration of the accumulation of tourists in time and space.

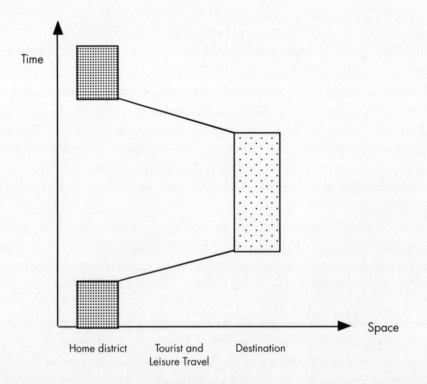

Figure 1.2. A time-geographical illustration of the formulation of the problem and its division into three parts: home district focusing on lifestyle in relation to leisure activities, tourism and leisure travel, and the impact on the destination.

studied from various angles. Sustainable tourism development is, then, a matter of attaching equal importance to the geographical, physical and ecological aspects of the environment and also the social and cultural ones as to the economic dimension of tourism. It is also essential not to see tourism as an isolated phenomenon but to place it in a social context. Further, in any discussion on sustainable development, the whole tourism system should be used as the point of departure, i.e. the demand, where lifestyle and consumer behaviour play a decisive role; tourism and leisure travel; and the destination, with its various types of carrying capacity. When the choices made by individuals, each of which taken separately may seem harmless, are aggregated in time and space, they may result in a serious impact on the environment (see Figure 1.1). One example of this is travelling from Europe on an ecotourist trip to Australia. The trip, we might think, is eco-labelled through its name. However, if many people make long journeys by air, the aircraft's fuel consumption and pollution are significant. Another example is the seasonal accumulation of many people in one area. In a sensitive area of the countryside this might lead to littering and damage.

AIM AND ISSUES

The initial formulation of the issue implies that the world is today facing environmental problems of an extent and character which have not occurred before. Tourism and leisure travel are expanding activities and are very widespread in the global community. Tourism and leisure activities, in their turn, have a varying impact on the environment.

The present study is limited to three aspects of the sustainability of tourism and leisure travel (see Figure 1.2): lifestyle in relation to tourism and leisure activities, tourism and leisure travel, and the impact on the destination. The aim is thus to identify non-sustainable elements in tourism and leisure activities and to study the possibility of more sustainable tourism development than is the case at present.

The fundamental features of this study are the environmental aspects as seen from the perspective of a social scientist. This is particularly emphasized in the sections dealing with lifestyle in relation to leisure activities involving mobility. It is primarily in the analysis of the significance and consequences of tourism at the destination that the concept of sustainability is expanded. In this context tourism will also be considered from a social and cultural as well as from an economic perspective.

The overarching questions which the study considers are primarily answered on the basis of data on the population of Sweden. However, the analysis and theoretical discussions are in large part generally valid for many rich countries. The study attempts to answer the following questions:

- What is the lifestyle of the Swedish population in connection with tourism and leisure activities and what are the indicators of that lifestyle?
- What links are there between the recreational lifestyle of Swedes and mobility?
- What is the significance from the perspective of environmental sustainability of the lifestyle of Swedes and their mobility in connection with leisure activities?
- How can sustainable tourism development be achieved at the destination?

In general terms, the concept of lifestyle may be said to consist of two parts: people's values and attitudes, and how we actually reveal our lifestyle through our behaviour. In this study lifestyle is limited to the latter and, in particular, to people's activities during their leisure time which can primarily be measured in terms of the use of time.

THE DATA

Various kinds of data are used in the study. The material will be presented in more detail later. First, I have gained a comprehensive pre-understanding of the problem area through a study of the international literature in the form of books and journals, through participation in international conferences and through personal contacts.

Second, the time-use study carried out by Statistics Sweden in 1990–91, and studies of the use of leisure time related to living conditions will form a basis for analysing lifestyle in terms of the use of time during leisure and its importance for sustainable tourism development. This material is complemented in some cases with secondary material.

Third, I have made a study of the programme 'A Sustainable Värmland' (in the province of Värmland, Sweden). This programme is being run by the organization Miljöaktion Värmland (Environmental Action in Värmland). The study includes Miljöaktion Värmland together with the bodies who fund its activities. To be more precise, I have analysed their policy documents and certain of their studies in the field of sustainable development, welfare and environment in the period 1990–95.

THE RESEARCH PROCESS AND TIME-GEOGRAPHY

The approach underpinning the study is as follows. First, the study is imbued with a time-geographical perspective. Second, the study has been conducted in accordance with an abductive research process. Third, sustainable tourism development is seen as part of a wider approach involving sustainable development in general. Fourth and finally, it has been my intention that sustainable tourism development should cover all forms of tourism, from mass tourism to small-scale tourism and specialized forms.

I would describe my own research process as primarily abductive. Today the abductive research process is, in many cases, seen as a more exact description of the research process than induction and deduction, in particular as regards case-study based surveys (Alvesson and Sköldberg 1994). The abductive process can start either with uninterpreted empirical material or with a pre-understanding of material that has already been interpreted. The approach entails choosing a particular issue as the point of departure, then collecting, processing and categorizing data to form hypothetical patterns and thereby developing a theory. This process may well give rise to new questions which, in their turn, require a different method for studying qualitatively different phenomena, thus commencing a new process of collecting, categorizing and analysing data. These processes, including comparative analyses of the various data collections, continue until the data begin to form an overall pattern or theory generation (Starrin *et al.* 1991). To put it another way, the comparative analyses help clarify the relationships that create a theory. Furthermore, theory generation is an endless process. It should always be possible to adjust and alter the theory. The process is dialectic and entails an alternation between part and whole (Starrin and Svensson 1994, p. 26).

There are a number of reasons for describing the present study as abductive. The original and overarching question we asked was: What is sustainable tourism development? This question resulted in various surveys based on different sets of data, which were all used in an attempt to provide as good an overall illustration of the issue as possible. As regards the breadth of approach in terms of methods and surveys, the study includes everything from a time-use survey of a quantitative type to a qualitative textual analysis. Another example of the abductive process is the scrutiny of the various parts of the tourism system in relation to the whole. Further, the lifestyle of the tourist in itself forms a entity but may at the same time be looked upon as part of larger entities – the tourism system and tourism in the life of the community. Parts and wholes are thus to be found at various levels.

Time-geography, which is the main perspective of the study and of whose methods I have made partial use, can be seen as an alternation between method and perspective. When I speak of methods in time-geography, I mean that, from my perspective, time-geography has a main method, which may be described as the science of putting things together to enable processes to be described and analysed in time and space (Åquist 1992, 1994, pp. 129–35; Hallin 1988, pp. 32–52, 1991, pp. 199–207). Thus time-geography reveals a composite flow of people's individual paths, of material flows etc. in space–time (Ellegård 1990). For me time-geography, apart from providing a method and a language for revealing the basic links in the relationship between people and the environment, also involves a perspective. This perspective is theoretical in nature and difficult to seize upon. It probably finds its best expression in the many research papers by Torsten Hägerstrand (Carlestam and Sollbe 1991; Ellegård 1983, 1991; Hägerstrand 1977, 1985, 1989). I shall not attempt to describe it in detail but simply say that it provides a good holistic view of the relationship between people and the environment, based on fundamental conditions in time and space, and through its concentration on changes in physical/material space. Torsten Hägerstrand provides the following clarification in a letter where he says that time-geography is a way of approaching the physical everyday world.[4]

> by which I mean that it is based on the material nature of the world (a side that is neglected by humanists and social scientists). Some years ago I came across a better way of formulating the forms of knowledge we are dealing with in the work of the Finnish philosopher Eino Kaila. He speaks about the physicalistic world = the one which physicists have constructed by means atoms, molecules, crystals, genes, gravitation, electromagnetic forces etc., and the physical everyday world = land, trees, houses, table, chairs etc. Time-geography is a way of approaching the physical everyday world (which has always been the geographers' field) with the addition that nature also has an everyday world (observe a bird looking for something to eat) and that man has a body to cope with. As regards the mental aspects, I am inclined to agree with the American psychologist, James Gibson, who writes 'Ask not what's inside your head, but what your head's inside of.' In this sense, the most general explanation of what people are doing is that they are imitating others without thinking too much about it. Pioneers are few and far between. I think this is true of tourism as well. But I admit that my ontology is unusual and a major shift of perspective is necessary in order to grasp the picture of reality that time-geography is attempting to provide. Above all, we must get behind the treacherous categorizations of verbal language. (my translation)

My intention is not to separate method and perspective in time-geography and erect watertight barriers between them, since I do not see this school in those terms. The reason for pointing out that there is both a method and a perspective is that it makes the parallels with the abductive research process visible. In this study I attempt to relate the time-geographical method to the time-geographical perspective as a whole.

CHAPTER 2

What Is Sustainable Tourism Development? – An Orientation

INTRODUCTION

Across the World, the use of the term 'sustainable' has become widespread, and fashionable, so that it is in danger of becoming meaningless. Often, it is not defined, and used in so many different ways that it clearly does not reflect a consensus in meaning. (Travis 1992, p. 4)

As the above quotation shows, it is important to try and define the concept of sustainable tourism development. The following section will provide a theoretical survey of:

- what tourism is
- the concept of development
- sustainable development
- sustainable tourism development.

For obvious reasons sustainable tourism development will be discussed in more detail later in the study.

WHAT IS TOURISM?

General

Tourism consists of a multitude of different types of journeys. In the following I shall discuss some definitions and classifications of tourism travel which are of value in this context. Basically, tourism is a movement in space from a person's home district to one or more destinations and then back again. Implicit in the definition is the idea of being away from home for a certain period of time. Most definitions tend to specify an absence both of a certain minimum time, e.g. 24 hours, and of a certain maximum time, e.g. one year. A distance criterion is also implied; for example, one of the categories in the survey of travel habits carried out by Statistiska Centralbyrån in 1994 was leisure travel farther than 100 km from one's home. The rich variety of definitions of tourism include many other criteria, for instance that the absence from home is voluntary and that the money spent at the destination has not been earned there (Cohen 1974; Ogilvie 1933). Apart from these, there is often a classification of the aims and motives for the journey.

The definition formulated by the World Tourism Organization (WTO) for domestic tourism is one of the most commonly used for operational purposes and contains many of the above criteria (the definition of international tourism is similar). It is as follows:

> a traveller visiting a destination in his country of residence for at least 24 hours but less than one year for the purpose of recreation, holidays, sport, business, meetings, conventions, study, visiting friends or relatives, health, mission work, or religion. (WTO in Smith, S. L. J. 1989, p. 20)

An important aim of this study is to demonstrate the significance of lifestyle for tourism. As Frändberg puts it:

> The conditions and reasons for tourism cannot really be found in the places that tourists visit. With this point of departure, it may be argued instead that resources for tourism are created by the conditions existing in the places that the tourists temporarily leave or perhaps rather by the contrast between 'home' and 'away.' (Frändberg 1993, p. 11, my translation)

In its turn, the tourism system reveals the structural framework of tourism and also the way in which tourism is embedded in the overall social system. The 'internal' tourism system can be described in terms of the mutual dependence between supply and demand. In its turn, the tourism system forms part of the economic, political, social, cultural and ecological systems and conditions, which influence its extent, content and structure, and also the sustainability aspects of tourism and leisure travel within the social system. To put it briefly, the tourism system is part of the overall social system (cf. Aronsson, 1994).

Among other things, this study will deal with the leisure activities of the Swedish people, of which tourism is a subset. Further, I shall present a number of theoretical arguments on tourism, primarily leisure tourism. It is the 'freedom' from the rules of society during leisure that is seen as problematic in the

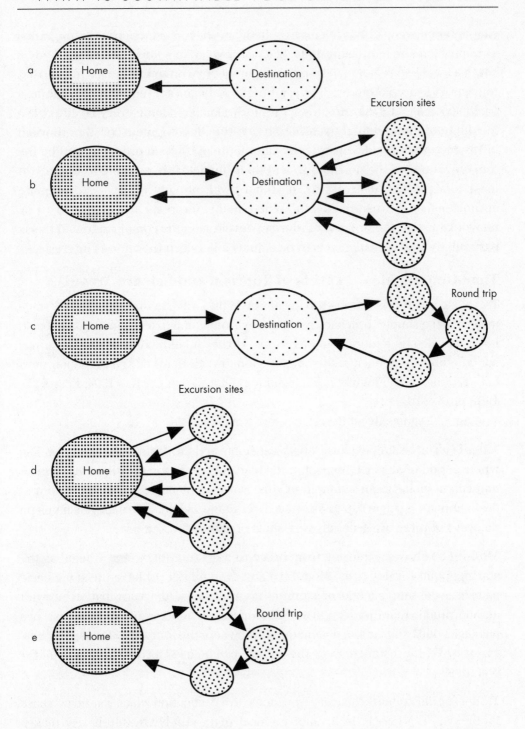

Figure 2.1. Models of tourism travel.

encounter between different cultures. In this respect, business trips are regarded as unproblematic (Svalastog 1994, p. 4). Moreover, in some parts of the study, I adopt a local and regional development perspective on tourism. This means that tourism is synonymous with everything that is connected with tourism in a particular area. In this sense, then, the study also covers the everyday life of the local population, which is affected by the development of the tourism infrastructure at the destination, by the supply of tourism products, and by the tourists who visit the destination and their impact. It is possible to identify at least four groups of actors at the local level, namely tourists, developers, authorities and local residents. When many interests are involved, it is unavoidable that the process of tourism development is complicated and this is particularly true if a balance is to be achieved between the various interests.

Time-Geographical Aspects of Tourism and Leisure Travel

Travelling as a tourist means leaving an (invisible) trace in time–space. This trace may have the simple form such as a journey from home to a destination and back, but it can also take more complex forms. However, all models of tourism travel contain three components: the home region, the destination(s) and the journeys between them (cf. Flognfeldt jr. 1993; Flognfeldt jr. and Onshus 1996; Pearce, D. 1987, pp. 5–20).

Figure 2.1 shows five different types of travel models.

Model (a) is the simple journey between home and the destination and back. The whole period of absence is spent at the place of recreation (destination) or in its immediate vicinity. An example of this type is a package holiday at a tourist destination or a single trip to a cottage over the weekend. There may be stops on the way but these are generally very short breaks in the journey.

Model (b) shows a journey from home to a destination which is used as the starting-point for day trips. Model (b) and even model (c) have the same basic pattern as the simple model of a journey between home and a destination but with an additional travel pattern at the destination. The example in this case is a package holiday by air to a destination from where the tourist makes trips by bus, car or cycle, for instance. Even the cottage can be used as the starting-point for day trips.

Model (c) illustrates the journey from home to a destination which is used as a base for the visit. This base is the location for much of the visit but the tourist also makes a round trip. An example of this is the unorganized (individual) package holiday where the traveller flies to a destination and uses it as the starting-point for a round trip by bus or car for instance, returning to the initial destination to fly home.

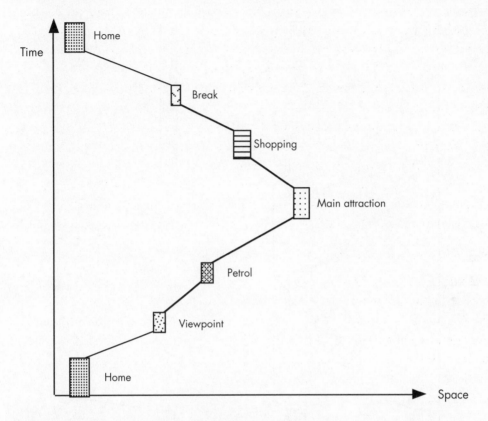

Figure 2.2. A time-geographical illustration of a day trip starting from home.

Model (d) shows the individual's home town as the starting-point for separate journeys and excursions during a leisure period. These are often short journeys, either day or weekend trips. Various forms of transport may be used.

Model (e) illustrates a round trip with overnight stays using one's home as the point of departure. There is no main destination. The individual places included in the round trip are just places the traveller passes through. Round trips by car with or without a caravan and bus trips are examples of this type of travel. Bus trips are often planned in detail whilst car trips do not have to be. The stops the traveller makes vary between short breaks for petrol to visits to attractions and overnight stays.

The models presented in Figure 2.1 illustrate the spatial dimension of the tourist's journeys but the time dimension is not shown. In Figure 2.2 I include the time dimension for a tourist trip, which produces a more realistic illustration than the very general travel models in Figure 2.1. The time-geographically illustrated journey in Figure 2.2 corresponds to model (e) in Figure 2.1, i.e. a day trip starting from home.

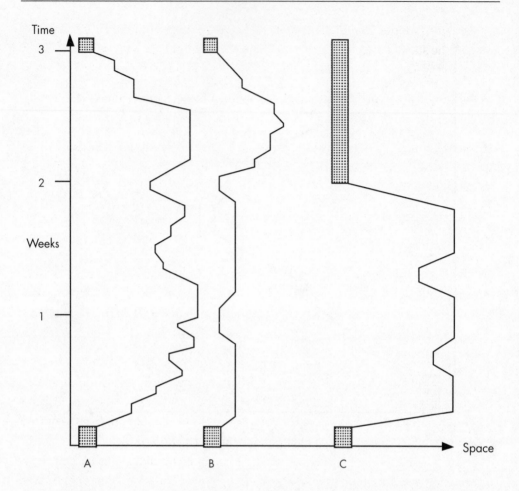

Figure 2.3. An outline figure combining a life-cycle perspective with various forms of transport and a created time–space structure for different tourist journeys.

Furthermore, in a time-geographical outline figure it is possible to combine demographic or other factors with the time–space structure. Figure 2.3 reproduces the combination of life-cycle perspective, various forms of transport and a created time–space structure for different tourist journeys. The following types of journeys are illustrated in Figure 2.3:

A = Individual in a group of young people. Type of journey: interrailing in Europe. Travel model: round trip starting from home. Transport: train. Length of journey: three weeks.

B = Middle-aged family with small children. Type of travel: initially a visit to a weekend cottage on two occasions during the same leisure period, then a holiday by car. Travel model: home as the starting-point – journey to the destination; and home as the starting-point – round trip. Transport: car and car with caravan. Length of journey: Weekend cottage not quite two weeks and travel holiday about a week.

C = Retired family. Type of travel: package holiday. Travel model: home – destination and two excursions. Transport: air and bus. Length of journey: two weeks.

From the tourist's point of view there are a number of conditions that have to be met before he or she makes the journey or, in other words, there are a number of restrictions on travelling.

1. The tourist must be interested in travelling.
2. The tourist's physical and mental health or ill health places a limitation on activities.
3. The time at the disposal of the tourist (day trips, weekend journey and a holiday trip).
4. Space is a restrictive factor where the range is decided by the form of transport and infrastructure.
5. Economic means at the disposal of the tourist.

Apart from these points, the amount of time required is determined by the object of the journey and the activities the tourist intends to carry out. Visiting an event in another place than one's home town, for instance, probably requires less time than a composite objective of visiting a number of attractions in different places over a certain period of time. Jansson discusses the tourists' various time-geographical prisms or as he puts it 'the tourist's scope for activities and its restrictions' (Jansson 1994, pp. 87–93, my translation). He uses a figure to show the limits of time–space for the tourist with a given form of transport (see Figure 2.4). The amount of time required and the costs of owning and/or using various forms of transport differ. Walking, cycling, travelling by car or flying create different prisms for the individual or provide different ranges in time–space. Even the individual's socio-economic situation, e.g. access to money, creates different prisms, and, in their turn, these may determine the form of transport or the possibility of visiting relations and friends in other places.

Compared to the train, the car is a more flexible means of transport for most destinations today and, furthermore, it is more convenient as it can carry luggage from door to door. Representatives of the tourism industry, for instance, often stress the importance of flexibility in the tourist's choice of transport. However, it may be asked what the environmental effects are of unlimited flexibility and mobility in tourism and leisure activities.

From the perspective of sustainable tourism development, we may ask whether

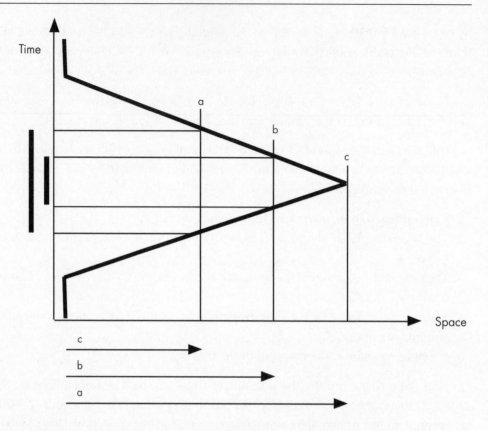

Figure 2.4. 'The limits of time–space. The figure shows the limits of time–space starting from home. **a** shows its ultimate limit, i.e. the distance one can travel and still get back home before the leisure period is over. **b** and **c** are examples of the limit that is set by the need to remain at the destination for a certain length of time for the visit to be meaningful. One might say that **b** and **c** exemplify the limits on the individual's practical scope for action.'
Source: Jansson (1994, p. 90)

the planning authorities should create more favourable conditions or introduce restrictions so that the individual chooses the form of transport that has the least negative effects on the environment. Another alternative would be to favour the development of a structure for activities and products in the local environment in order to reduce travel. A further issue concerns the use of land for developing the infrastructure for various forms of transport and the consequent impact of this on the environment. There is a further dimension to sustainable development apart from the physical and ecological ones referred to above and that is the welfare dimension. Which people are favoured and which are not if the conditions are changed or restrictions introduced to achieve more sustainable development?

A structural development of tourism and leisure activities in the local environment should favour disadvantaged groups by reducing travel costs. The disabled may, on the other hand, be at a disadvantage if restrictions on motor traffic are introduced in an area or if flexibility in the choice of transport is reduced. Most of the questions raised above will be dealt with in more detail later.

THE CONCEPT OF DEVELOPMENT

The concept of development has long been the subject of lively debate and a number of schools have emerged (Aronsson 1989, pp. 53–65). The term is used in many everyday contexts, such as development for an individual, an organization, a place or for society as a whole. But what do we mean by development? The simplest definition is that development means change. However, this is not completely self-evident. Frängsmyr (in Hettne 1982, p. 176) points out that development may mean different things but it is generally associated with positive social change, which means moving forward to something that is better than the present. Again it is not self-evident that this is the case. There are, for instance, different opinions about how best to measure development and about what the measurement in fact says. Furthermore, several schools have emerged since the Second World War, such as the school of growth and modernization, Marxism, and the dependency school, and development from above or below (Blomström and Hettne 1981; Friedmann and Weaver 1979; Hettne 1982; Mabogunje 1980; Stöhr and Taylor 1981; Wahlström 1984).[5]

Society may be studied in terms of different but mutually dependent sub-systems. These have various spatial foundations and domains of influence. Does economic growth automatically mean positive development in the social and ecological systems as well? It is clear that this cannot be taken for granted. Development is also a question of scale. Positive developments at the macro level are, for instance, not automatically positive for households and individuals at the micro level. Most intentions from above have unexpected and unplanned side-effects (Andersson 1987, 1991; cf. Hägerstrand 1984, p. 17). Do these unexpected effects result from the fact that all too often social planning is seen from a functional perspective? In this approach one selects a function or section of the whole without indicating the whole and without putting the part back into the whole again later. To take an example, a study is made of the air pollution caused by motor vehicles. The results are then used to speed up technical solutions such as catalysts for cleaning exhaust fumes, or closing certain streets to motor traffic. An alternative approach is to describe and analyse the context, the traffic system that people have created, make sub-surveys of the consequences of this system, provide solutions from a holistic perspective and finally go back to the beginning: what would be the consequences for people's lifestyle? It might be interesting to keep the different possible meanings of development in mind. It might also be useful to ask the following questions: development for whom, how and to what?

SUSTAINABLE DEVELOPMENT

The concept of sustainable development has gained real meaning since the publication of the report *Our Common Future*, by the World Commission on Environment and Development, also known as the Brundtland Commission (Hägerhäll 1988). Sustainable development can be traced back to the schools mentioned above, in particular to the debate on resources in the study *The Limits to Growth* (Meadows *et al.* 1972) and the UN symposium on the relation between resources, environment and development which was held in Stockholm in 1979. There are traces of all the above schools of thought in the Brundtland report apart perhaps from the pure growth school. Despite this collection of earlier ideas, sustainable development as a concept has enough substance to enable it to be defined itself as a school of thought in development theory. The Brundtland report provides the following content for sustainable development (Hägerhäll 1988, pp. 22–3):

- People themselves have the capacity to achieve sustainable development.
- A long-term perspective is necessary; there must be sufficient resources and a good environment for coming generations as well.
- There must be a balance between rich and poor countries; everybody's basic needs must be provided for.
- We must all, in the rich world in particular, change our attitudes and lifestyles to favour sustainable ecologically adapted development.
- Development is a process that can be steered towards sustainability.

The United Nations Conference on Environment and Development (UNCED) in Rio de Janeiro in 1992 took the discussion on sustainable development further. This gathering consisted of a formal conference with representatives of about 180 governments and a parallel alternative conference of non-governmental organizations, called the Global Forum. One of the most important documents to emerge from the conference was Agenda 21. This 'plan of action for the future' covers many of the areas affected by environmental issues. The idea is that the municipality level together with representatives of industry, organizations and the inhabitants should plan for the next century on the basis of the Rio declaration.[6]

There was agreement at the conference that during 1993 the UN would establish a 'Commission for Sustainable Development' with the aim of supervising the implementation of the measures adopted by the Rio conference.

The Rio conference has been criticized for watering down the text of the documents; there has also been criticism of the fact that sustainable development for the rich world means maintaining 'the conditions that allow continued growth in the economy in order to conserve today's lifestyle' (Kohr 1992, p. 2, my translation), which includes preserving the current world order and the consumer patterns of the rich world. The criticism concerns the fact that environmental issues must be integrated with issues of social justice, human rights and development at all levels (Kohr 1992, pp. 2–5). In terms of development theory, this criticism can be traced back to the dependency school's argument that socio-economic conditions are built into the centre–periphery relation. On the positive side, the Rio conference highlighted the issue of the global environment and development, and most of the participating countries did, in fact, sign the documents that were produced, which shows that there was considerable agreement on the lowest common denominator in environmental and development issues.

I would like to add a few comments to the above discussion. As I see it, there are two ways of approaching sustainable development. One is based on the view that species and ecosystems have a value in themselves and should be allowed to exist on their own terms (Næss 1992, pp. 1–5), whilst the other centres on human beings and implies that even if the other species have the right to exist, it is the survival of humans that is superordinate. Reflecting an anthropocentric perspective, the Rio declaration states that: 'the human being is at the heart of our concerns for sustainable development and that each has the right to a healthy and productive life in contact with nature' (Baltscheffsky 1992, p. 7, my translation).

Furthermore, there are two seemingly paradoxical aspects to sustainable development, namely conservation and development. Thus it is a matter of preserving, for instance, the wealth of species in a natural area and, at the same time, striving for development in a society in order to attain the goals of greater welfare for the people. Svalastog discusses these aspects and shows how the concept of sustainable development can be used in a more or less radical sense (cf. Sandell 1996b).

I. The term sustainable development has the following two main dimensions:

– A resource dimension associated with the long-term use and development of the local countryside and local culture.

– A dimension associated with workplaces and material rewards. The rewards may be sufficient to provide a basis for establishing family-firms and for generation shifts.

II. The three schools:

There is no clear agreement on what is an optimal and (ethically) defensible use of resources over time. We can therefore speak of the following three schools in this area.

Alternative 1. The simplest definition of sustainable development is the optimal use of resources over time for the good of the people who have access to the resources. The central argument here is that over time people will exploit the resources as much as possible without regard to the consequences for natural and cultural variety.

Alternative 2. A second school also argues for the greatest possible exploitation of resources over time but only on condition that the natural and cultural variety is preserved. This school believes that it is essential to preserve the natural and cultural variety to ensure long-term survival, stability and richness of experience. This standpoint has a more solid scientific basis than the first but it has been attacked by social scientists as well as by philosophers and humanists. The approach works primarily in political contexts as long as the superordinate policy goal is to maximize consumption within a political unit in the short and medium term.

Alternative 3. A third school, which is an extension of the second, maintains explicitly that the consumption of resources must be seen in a global context. In other words, consumption must not be so great as to harm societies in other parts of the world. (Here we have an example of the centre/periphery dimension between rich and poor and between centre and periphery in a country. Increased consumption in the rich parts of the world cannot be reconciled with sustainable development since it results in the poor countries being underpaid for the raw materials they export or in environmentally hostile industries, which the rich countries do not want, being located within their borders.) From an ethical and social science standpoint it is claimed that this is the only defensible definition of sustainable development. (Svalastog 1996, my translation)

The perspective applied in Parts I, II and III of the present study is primarily that of the third school in Svalastog's classification, whilst in Part IV, which is locally oriented and has a bias towards production theory, the perspective is rather that of the second school (see the quotation above).

If we consider Swedish conditions and, primarily, the ecological sub-system, Swedish environmental goals are nowadays expressed in terms of the tolerance limits for various substances, which, in their turn, are linked to conditions in the

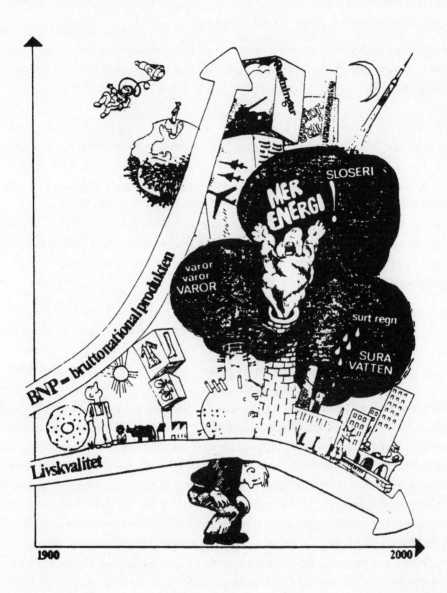

Figure 2.5. A Swedish interpretation of the background to the discussion on sustainable development. The figure shows the increasing discrepancy between economic development, on the one hand, and environmental problems and problems related to the development of civil society, on the other.
Source: Miljötidningen (1978)

various regions. According to Miljödepartementet (Department of the Environment) the environmental goals are as follows:

- To safeguard the continued existence of the human race, its health and well-being. Pollution must not be permitted to constitute a threat to the reproductive capacity and health of mankind, either in the present generation or in future ones.
- To preserve the variety of life. The species which exist in the country will be able to develop in the long term, primarily in the areas where they are found at present.
- To achieve long-term conservation and utilization of natural resources. Forestry, agriculture and fishing must be maintained on a very long-term basis.
- To preserve the natural and cultural landscape and cultural monuments. Pollution must not be permitted to destroy buildings and objects. The availability of valuable natural and cultural landscapes must not be significantly reduced. (Miljödepartementet 1991, p. 8, my translation)

The presentation and discussion in this section very clearly show the great complexity of the concept of sustainable development and the underlying criticism of documents dealing with it. One of the most important conclusions, as I see it, is that the concept must be set in the context of a development theory tradition in order to be really understood. It may also be concluded that the political system must provide the visions, and influence the systems of rules and rewards to achieve local participation in decisions if we are to attain a more sustainable world in the future. In this context we might consider the discussion on development from above or from below, where it is asked with what group or level in society power and initiative should rest. Further, in order to achieve sustainable development, the economic system must be oriented towards, possibly even regulated in terms of, environmental values, aspects of global distribution, and so forth. The social and cultural systems, where individuals are considered as a collective, must change their ethic and become better adapted to the environment (cf. World Commission on Culture and Development 1996). Finally, an explanation of the various interpretations of sustainable development is to be found in the differences in the depth of radicalization among those using the term, as is shown in the above quotation from Svalastog.

SUSTAINABLE TOURISM DEVELOPMENT

The world conference on 'Sustainable Tourism' on Lanzarote in the spring of 1995 was a thematic successor to the Rio conference. Its organizers declared:

> The application of the principles of the Rio Declaration to tourism development is of fundamental strategic value, in view of the importance of tourism. The growing specific weight of tourism as a major consumer of natural resources in the world economy is beyond dispute.[7]

The conference, which attracted about six hundred delegates, was both a conference and a forum. The forum contained a large number of presentations and some exhibitions. The conference resulted in two documents: 'Charter for Sustainable Tourism' and 'The Sustainable Tourism Plan of Action'. These documents were addressed to the governments of the world, other decision-makers, organizations connected with tourism, and professionals in the field. The Charter for Sustainable Tourism is a declaration which sets out eighteen principles for how tourism should be controlled so that it can be included in the global strategy for sustainable development. The Sustainable Tourism Plan of Action outlines the special strategies and proposals for action to be developed by those signing the declaration.[8] In the declaration's first principle an attempt is made to define or to indicate what sustainability for tourism entails: 'Tourism development shall be based on criteria of sustainability, which means that it must be ecologically bearable in the long term, economically viable, as well as ethically and socially equitable for the local communities.'[9]

I shall not consider the eighteen principles in detail, but merely mention some basic points. As was implied above, safeguarding the cultural heritage and the natural environment at tourist destinations is most important and support should be given to those areas which are already at risk of being damaged by tourism. Special priority should be given to the most sensitive areas, for instance small islands, mountain areas and historical sites. In general, the declaration attaches great importance to the interests of the local communities but it should also be noted that the need for the cooperation of and contributions from actors at various levels is underlined, in particular from non-governmental organizations. Tools for preserving and also for developing more sustainable tourism should be devised, but planning and management are also mentioned as well as the distribution of tourism over the whole year. Other aspects that are taken up include the need to change consumer patterns and to put a price on environmental resources in order to achieve a global reduction in their use. Alternative forms of tourism in line with the principles of sustainable tourism should be marketed to a greater extent. It is important for the tourism industry to develop and apply codes of ethics for sustainable tourism. Furthermore, the increase of knowledge (research), information networks on sustainable tourism and the implementation of sustainable tourism projects for demonstration purposes are also important. Finally, it should be noted that (only) one of the eighteen principles mentions the importance of the environmental impact of the transport system for tourism and the need to develop instruments to reduce the use of non-renewable energy sources.

In the following, I shall attempt to classify the large number of papers presented during the forum. The classification is based on the three parts of the tourism system indicated in Figure 1.2. There was relatively little discussion of the first part, research on the lifestyle of the tourist, background factors, conditions and restrictions for tourist activities, only approximately one tenth of the papers. The second, travel, was dealt with to an even lesser extent. I did not find one paper whose main objective was a study of the impacts on energy consumption and the environment of tourist travel. 'The notion of sustainable tourism has grown out of a response to our overt failures to deal with the random mal-effects of inappropriate tourism development on the environments which host it' (Travis 1992, p. 1).

This quotation could be used to illustrate the topics covered by the vast majority of the presentations at the Lanzarote conference. There was a marked emphasis on the various impacts on tourist destinations, most attention being given to ecological and physical impacts and then, in descending order, to social and cultural impacts, including aspects of local participation in the development of tourism (political impacts) and finally to local economic impacts. This concentration on destination research and the effects of tourism on destinations was also highlighted in the principles in the Charter for Sustainable Tourism. The presentations covered case-studies from many parts of the world but there was little attempt at generating theory.

Other themes were also represented in the papers at the Lanzarote conference and also influenced the principles in the declaration. I would like to make a few comments on them.

There are many examples around the world of places and areas which have developed mass tourism. Mass tourism moves in a north-south direction across the globe and the destination countries are greater in number and more widely spread than the tourist-generating countries (Smith and Eadington 1992, p. 5). As Hall puts it: 'destination countries represent a much wider spread than originating countries, reflecting a spatial diffusion of tourists from the developed world across the globe, with fastest growth in the more remote regions of the Third World.' (Hall, D. 1994, p. 540)

People's search for unspoilt nature or older socio-cultural environments leads them to travel farther and farther afield – to the peripheral (Frändberg 1996, p. 5). One of the reasons for the increasingly longer journeys is that industrialism and modernity are penetrating further and further into the remote areas of the world. Apart from the fact that tourism is a leading factor for change in these environments, the consequences of this are the high level of energy consumption and global environmental impacts. The question is whether mass tourism is sustainable in the long term and, in that case, where does this sustainability occur? Is the economy produced by tourism sustainable? Are the changes in the social and cultural structures and in the natural environment desirable and acceptable? In the papers given at the Lanzarote conference the answer to all these questions was 'No'. The consequences of a move towards mass tourism are often clearer in countries with a lower economic and material standard of welfare than in countries in rich world. Thus, examples of tourism development from these areas often provide good illustrations. Concentrating studies of tourism on economically poor countries underlines the fact that much of the tourism travel to these countries leads to cultural collisions and a form of neo-colonialism in that most of the economic effects of tourism flow back to the rich world, primarily through the international companies that own and run the tourism industry. Most of the remaining income goes to the upper-class in the poor countries (Høivik and Heiberg 1977; Lea 1988; Rossel 1988). This reasoning suggests that the inhabitants of the rich world should restrict their tourist travel to their own cultural sphere. Is sustainable tourism from rich to poor countries not conceivable, or are there forms, such as ecotourism, which constitute an exception? The issue of specialized forms of tourism, e.g. ecotourism, and their relation to sustainable tourism development, will be discussed in more detail later.

Sustainable tourism development may be interpreted in a narrow and a broad sense (cf. Hunter 1995). The narrow definition is basically limited to the tourism system and is less related to the surrounding social system. The broad definition establishes a clear link between tourism and the social system. The following quotation demonstrates a relatively narrow interpretation of sustainable tourism development:

> In the case of the tourism industry, sustainable development has a fairly specific meaning – the industry's challenge is to develop tourism's capacity and the quality of its products without adversely affecting the physical and human environment that sustains and nurtures them. (Cronin in Hunter and Green 1995, p. 70)

To summarize, the following points are emphasized in a broad and prescriptive interpretation of sustainable tourism development (cf. de Kadt 1992, p. 50; Pigram 1992, p. 78):

- Tourism development may take place if it does not damage the environment and is ecologically sound.
- Sustainable tourism development largely consists of small-scale development and is based on the local community.
- Sustainable tourism development takes its point of departure in who benefits from tourism. The aim is not to exploit the local residents.
- Sustainable tourism development places the emphasis on cultural sustainability, e.g. the destination is developed in such a way that the feel of the place is retained in its architecture and cultural heritage.

SOME INTERNATIONAL EXAMPLES OF PROJECTS INVOLVING THE ADAPTATION OF TOURISM TO THE ENVIRONMENT

Agenda 21 for the Travel and Tourism Industry

Together with the Earth Council and the World Tourism Organization, the World Travel and Tourism Council has designed an Agenda 21 for the travel and tourism industry. This specific Agenda 21 takes up a number of points relating to the adaptation of tourism to the environment. If a tourism company adopts and follows the points given below, it will be included in the World Travel and Tourism Council's environmental classification in accordance with the so-called 'Green Globe'. Agenda 21 for the travel and tourism industry includes the following points:

- Waste – minimize, re-use and recycle.
- Energy – save and use effectively, reduce emissions.
- Fresh water resources – safeguard quality, avoid waste.
- Drainage water – purify and reduce effluent.
- Environmentally dangerous substances – replace such products.
- Transport – avoid harmful pollution and other impacts on the environment.
- Use of land – plan, look after, prevent the uglification of the landscape.
- Involve employees, customers and local receivers.
- Design products and techniques so they are more efficient, less polluting, locally appropriate and globally available.
- Cooperation – with the local communities, tourists, small enterprises, sectoral bodies, the local councils, the government. (Hanneberg 1996, p. 58, my translation)

Beatha – Environmental Quality Mark

Together with interest groups in Ireland, the European Union is developing a new environmental policy entitled 'Beatha – Environmental Quality Mark' within the framework of the LIFE programme.[10] Beatha – Environmental Quality Mark is an environmental classification whose aim is to send a clear signal that a particular area has a very high quality environment which is worth visiting. The classification also shows that the particular area is being developed and managed so as to preserve the environment. In all development there should be a balance between human activities, economic development and protection of the environment through shared responsibility between different actors. The classification may be compared with the use of International Standards Organization standards in industry, where certain criteria must be met to obtain and retain the classification. What is new in this environmental policy is that it is based on three points of departure. The first is that even if improvements have been made in the environment within the European Union, there remains much to be done. The second is that the present economic development model cannot be used in the future since it is unsustainable. The third is that legislation alone cannot solve environmental problems. The economic sector and public authorities must share responsibility for the environment. The programme is being implemented in its first phase in Ireland. If it is successful there, it will be used through the European Union as a general classification for areas which have met the requirements for green tourism.

Towards Sustainable Tourism in Finland

One of the starting-points for the work of the Finnish Tourist Board is the fact that environmental problems in service industries such as tourism have attracted little interest in comparison with the problems caused by the manufacturing industry. Against this background and given the economic importance of tourism for Finland, efforts are being made to base tourism development on the idea of sustainability. The Tourist Board describes the goals of tourism development in the following terms:

> A responsible, forward-looking tourism policy provides incentives for protecting the natural and cultural environment, creates economic precon-ditions for restoration and preservation work, promotes regional development and helps keep local traditions alive. International tourism gives people of different nationalities a chance to find out more about one another and about different cultures and natural areas. Tourism offers opportunity to learn new things and have new experiences. (Finnish Tourist Board 1993, p. 1)

The Tourist Board notes that the greatest challenge in the present decade is to develop tourism that is adapted to sustainable development. The Board also points out that sustainable tourism development requires the cooperation of a number of different actors, primarily the tourism industry, authorities, tourists and the local inhabitants. An underlying motive for sustainable tourism development is that offering the experience of a good environment in both rural and urban areas will enable the tourism industry to increase its competitiveness. For instance, the Board suggests, the tourism company will be able to earn money through an increase in demand, but also through such things as energy-saving measures. Further, they have established a number of key principles for achieving sustainable tourism development:

- In all new investments in tourism, environmental aspects should be taken into account from the start. The solutions should be long-term.
- Local traditions should be respected, e.g. the architectural design should be in harmony with the environment, landscape and the local building tradition. Further, the construction material used should be eco-friendly; build in wood – avoid plastic.
- Traditional landscapes and the natural variety should be preserved.
- Traffic problems should be reduced as much as possible.
- Sustainable tourism entails using public transport to the greatest possible extent and transfer journeys should be organized in the form of group transports.
- Eco-friendly activities should be encouraged, e.g. cycling, riding, canoeing, camping, and horse and dog transport etc.
- The tourism industry should use local products as far as possible and local labour. This covers everything from souvenirs and food products to local guides.
- Tourism employees should receive education and information so that they are, in all respects, in harmony with sustainable tourism.
- In natural areas visitors should walk along prepared paths, and on guided tours tourists should be given information about the natural setting to increase their environmental awareness.
- When tourism products are marketed, the information that is given should be correct and environmental aspects should be emphasized. (Finnish Tourist Board 1993, pp. 3–4)

Apart from these key principles for sustainable tourism, the Board also provides practical instructions for sustainability for tourism companies. These cover water, energy and waste.

In 1993, the Finnish Tourist Board launched a project whose objectives were to provide guidelines for sustainable tourism development and to coordinate various projects on sustainable tourism and eco-labelling for the Finnish tourism industry.

In order to obtain the necessary information for the project, a number of so-called eco-audits were made with the object of finding answers to three questions: how tourism companies handled environmental issues, what the attitudes of employees, customers and other interest groups to environmental issues were, and how environmental issues could be handled better (Finnish Tourist Board *et al.* 1995). The audits thus concentrated on the environmental impacts of the companies and how these could be reduced.[11] Ten different tourism companies, including city hotels, spa hotels, farm tourism, camping sites and ski resorts, were selected for auditing. The results of the eco-audit proved to be positive. The companies audited made improvements in their use of resources and energy and in waste disposal, among other things. Another interesting point was the fact that they managed to reduce the time spent on these matters. The project also produced proposals for further measurements to improve environmental work.

The National Strategy for Ecotourism in Australia

Ecotourism is seen as a major potential for tourism in Australia (McIntyre 1994). The national strategy for ecotourism rests on two pillars. One is the proper management of the natural resources on which tourism is based, in order to preserve the conditions for tourism, and the other is the fact that ecotourism provides an opportunity for increasing income in the form of foreign currency and new jobs etc. The following definition is used in the national strategy: 'Ecotourism is nature-based tourism that involves education and interpretation of the natural environment and is managed to be ecologically sustainable' (Commonwealth Department of Tourism 1994, p. 17).

The definition covers a range of activities. Nature also includes culture in those cases where cultural activities are directly based on natural conditions. Ecotourism is seen as an integral and complementary aspect of all tourism. The vision behind the strategy for ecotourism in Australia is the following:

> Australia will have an ecologically and culturally sustainable ecotourism industry that will be internationally competitive and domestically viable. Ecotourism in Australia will set an international example for environmental quality and cultural authenticity while realizing an appropriate return to the Australian community and conservation of the resource. (Commonwealth Department of Tourism 1994, p. 1)

The strategy for ecotourism has been discussed by and has received support from most groups of actors affected by tourism development, e.g. the public and private sectors, non-profit associations and representatives of the aborigines. It constitutes a philosophy for planning, developing and administering ecotourism. All the states in the Commonwealth of Australia are preparing their own strategies and policy documents (cf. Policies of the Goss Government 1993).

The strategy deals with the advantages and disadvantages of ecotourism for the environment, the social and cultural system and the economy (Commonwealth Department of Tourism 1994, pp. 19–22). The planning, development and administration of ecotourism are assessed in terms of the extent to which the advantages outweigh the disadvantages. The national strategy for ecotourism lays down a number of goals and proposes a number of actions (Commonwealth Department of Tourism 1994, pp. 23–48).

1. The goal is to facilitate the application of ecologically sustainable principles in the tourism industry. The principles are: to improve the material and immaterial well-being of the local inhabitants; to preserve the natural resources for future generations; to protect the ecological variety and ecological systems; and, the global aspect, that tourism in Australia must not lead to unsustainable consequences for other countries.

2. Integrated regional planning. This should be based on ecologically sustainable principles and be carried out in cooperation between the regions. Further, the local population should be involved in the planning process in order to ensure that social and cultural aspects are taken into account etc.

3. The administration of natural resources. The management of natural resources and ecotourism can be mutually supportive in that ecotourism yields income and the management of natural resources provides tourism with knowledge and the opportunity for experiences. Among other things, zoning can be introduced in particularly sensitive areas.

4. The tourism industry should regulate ecotourism itself through authorization.

5. Infrastructure and facilities should be designed and placed so as to melt into the environment; this includes using local material, local labour and developing processes that are low in energy consumption. The infrastructure should not be developed in sensitive areas.

6. Systems for information about and the supervision of ecotourism. Methods should be developed for increasing knowledge and information about the impact of tourism and ecotourism, which is of value in the planning and decision-making processes.

7. Australia still has a largely unexploited potential for ecotourism, which should result in more extensive marketing. Marketing should be grounded in the ethical message of ecotourism.

8. The introduction of a general standard of good quality for the industry and a national system of authorization should raise the value of ecotourism products and, at the same time, minimize the impact of ecotourism.

9. Education in ecotourism. Better knowledge of the environment, for instance, will influence the behaviour of tourists and improve the service provided by the tourism industry.

10. Cultural variety is an integral part of the concept of ecotourism, which makes it possible for the aborigines to be involved in the development of ecotourism. The goal is thus to improve the opportunities for this group of people to be involved in or to run ecotourism activities.

11. The long-term viability of ecotourism. Ecotourism is often run on a small scale and based on personal service. This means that this form of tourism must charge a relatively high price for the services it sells. Various investments must be made, for instance through greater knowledge and cooperation, to guarantee the viability of ecotourism.

12. Ecotourism competes with other activities for resources and the use of land. The proposal is to create an impartial planning and decision-making process where the actors concerned have the opportunity to say how they believe the resources should be used.

Measures have been proposed for the implementation of all the twelve goals we have considered. (Commonwealth Department of Tourism 1994, pp. 49–52)

SOME SWEDISH EXAMPLES OF PROJECTS FOR ADAPTING TOURISM TO THE ENVIRONMENT[12]

The Work of Miljövårdsberedningen (Committee for Environmental Control) on Sustainable Tourism

Miljövårdsberedningen has been charged by the government with the task of proposing measures for the sustainable development of the country's mountain areas. The proposals should provide an overall picture of the various demands on the natural resources in these areas. The multi-user perspective that has been adopted includes the interests of tourism, the reindeer industry, the military and the local resident population. In order to carry out this commission, Miljövårds-beredningen set up a consultative committee with representatives of the authorities, the sectors and organizations concerned (Miljödepartementet, Miljövårdsberedningen 1995).

Apart from the above, Miljövårdsberedningen also held a round-table conference in 1994 on the public right of access and ways of achieving sustainable tourism in Sweden. The participants came from the tourism industry, authorities, environmental and agricultural organizations among others. After this meeting, Naturvårdsverket (National Environmental Protection Board) was commissioned by the government to present proposals and guidelines for the commercial use of the public right of access (Miljövårdsberedningen 1994; Naturvårdsverket 1995b).

In the following I shall mention some of the main ideas that emerged from the round-table conference. In its report from the conference Miljövårdsberedningen takes the Rio conference and the idea of designing forms of tourism that meet the demands of long-term sustainable development as its point of departure. It also emphasizes the significance of local efforts in the spirit of Agenda 21, partly as a continuation of the campaign 'Let the whole of Sweden live' and partly for their importance for tourism development. In this context the committee draws attention to the role of ecotourism in the development of rural areas and underlines the need to devise ethical rules and environmental criteria for the tourism industry. The report also contains a specially adapted version for the tourism industry of the ethical rules of the International Chamber of Commerce, which have been adopted by much of Swedish industry. However, I shall not discuss these here. It is also interesting to note that the report defines the content of sustainable tourism and presents a vision of tourism development in Sweden.

> Sustainable tourism is a matter of adopting the idea of recycling in all parts of the industry. The construction of hotels and the choice of heating systems must be in line with ecological thinking. When the tourists are at the resort, the industry must ensure that over-consumption, waste and pollution, which often cause problems as tourism increases, are reduced to a minimum. Tourism must be planned as a long-term project – not something that may be exploited for money in the short-term. All tourism, including package holidays/mass tourism, both can and must be much better adapted to the environment than it is today. An increase in the demand for ecotourism will probably lead to a greater environmental adaptation of mass tourism . . . In the long term all mass tourism that exploits nature should disappear and be replaced by ecotourism . . . Even minor adaptation to the environment would have a considerable effect since mass tourism is the sector which affects the environment most. (Miljövårdsberedningen 1994, p. 6, my translation)

The report also specifies the content of development strategies for local ecotourism. It underlines the importance of local participation and indicates that local Agenda 21 efforts should include a development strategy for ecotourism. In this context, the concept of ecotourism should be a label which guarantees an environmental profile for the tourism product, i.e. accommodation, transport, restaurants and cafés, and activities including souvenirs. It provides a number of examples of measures to ensure that the tourism product has an environmental profile. An independent assessment is suggested for possible eco-labelling.

The World Wide Fund for Nature and Environmentally Adapted Tourism and Ecotourism

The World Wide Fund for Nature (WWF) (World Wildlife Fund (WWF) in US and Canada) has published a document entitled 'WWF och turismen. Miljöanpassad turism och Ekoturism' (WWF and Tourism. Environmentally Adapted Tourism and Ecotourism) (World Wide Fund for Nature 1995). This document has been produced by a project group consisting of representatives of authorities, non-governmental organizations and the tourism industry among others. As is apparent from the title, a distinction is made between environmentally adapted tourism in general and ecotourism. Like all other industry, tourism must, the document states, be adapted to the environment. There will be a growing demand for this in the future. Adapting to the environment means that the whole travel industry, from large tour operators, specialist travel agents, bus companies, hotels, and so forth, to those responsible at the destinations, will have to take greater responsibility for the environment than today. The definition of ecotourism used by the World Wide Fund for Nature is the one which has been devised by The Ecotourism Society: 'Ecotourism implies responsible travel which contributes to the protection of natural environments and the well-being of the local residents' (World Wide Fund for Nature 1995, p. 3, my translation). The document further states that: 'Ecotourism is not a product, but an attitude. It is more a question of how and with what attitude one travels, than where one travels' (*ibid.*, my translation).

As was indicated above, ecotourism places demands on consumers and tour operators. Furthermore, ecotourism is a form of small-scale tourism which is based on natural and cultural preconditions and which does not destroy the resources underpinning tourism. Ecotourism should also entail development and welfare, e.g. in the form of local economic utility, employment, support for environmental protection, education and health care in the area visited by the tourist. The WWF points out that ecotourism, like the concept of sustainable tourism, is being watered down – much that is termed ecotourism is not serious. The WWF is striving to achieve an eco-labelling of ecotourism, which, in its turn, may lead to competitive advantages for tourism products that are awarded this label. The WWF has laid down ten so-called commandments for environmentally adapted tourism; these are:

1. Use resources so as to conserve them.
2. Reduce over-consumption and pollution.
3. Preserve variety.

4. Integrate tourism in local and national planning (this includes describing the environmental impacts – my comment).
5. Favour local economies.
6. Cooperate with the local population.
7. Consult all interest groups.
8. Train the staff (in environmental adaptation – my comment).
9. Market tourism in a responsible manner.
10. Carry out surveys and follow them up. (World Wide Fund for Nature 1995, p. 4, my translation)

The WWF has laid down the following requirements for journeys to be termed ecotourism (the ten commandments of ecotourism):

1. The ecological and social capacity shall be decisive . . . The size of the tourist group shall be determined by the sensitivity of the area to be visited.
2. All tour operators should appoint a person responsible for the environment and adopt an environmental plan . . . The aim is that everybody in the business shall be more eco-friendly – from office and booking office to hotels, journeys, buses, airlines, camping sites, safari jeeps etc.
3. Environmental measures also apply to sub-contractors at the destination.
4. Select environmentally adapted hotel facilities. In the choice of accommodation for visitors, efforts shall be made to favour environmentally adapted facilities with the smallest impact on the environment (energy, noise, waste, lavatories, composting, water consumption etc.). Moreover, the facilities should preferably be built according to local tradition, with local material and with as many local staff as possible.
5. Really knowledgeable guides are crucial.
6. Favour the local economy . . . purchase as many goods and services as possible locally and from locally owned firms . . . use local food and drink and thus avoid too many imported goods.
7. Influence the tourist to adopt a respectful attitude. Tourists shall be informed without unnecessary 'exoticism' and persuaded not to disrupt the local people and to adopt a respectful attitude towards them and their customs, culture and nature. Opportunities should be provided for dignified encounters between tourists and the local people . . .
8. Do not buy their lives! . . . do not buy things made from animals and plants threatened with extinction.
9. Ecotourism requires good information to be given to the tourists.
10. Ecotourism should contribute to environmental protection and local development. (World Wide Fund for Nature 1995, pp. 5–6, my translation)

Finally, the WWF puts forward a number of proposals for measures. These include the need for a Swedish society for ecotourism and the eco-labelling of journeys. The latter can, it is suggested, be linked to local Agenda 21 efforts in the municipalities. Further, the document states that ecotourism is the preferable form of tourism for environmentally protected areas and that it should play a greater role in aid organizations (World Wide Fund for Nature 1995, p. 7).

Svenska Turistföreningen's (The Swedish Tourist Association's) Environmentally Adapted Tourism and Ecotourism

Like the WWF, the Swedish Tourist Association (STF) distinguishes between the environmental adaptation of tourism and ecotourism. Environmentally adapted tourism is dealt with in 'STF Miljöprogram' (STF Environmental Programme) (Svenska Turistföreningen 1990) and in 'Miljöanpassad turism – ekoturism. Policyprogram för Svenska Turistföreningen' (Environmentally Adapted Tourism – Ecotourism. Policy Programme for the Swedish Tourist Association) (Svenska Turistföreningen 1994). Ecotourism is dealt with briefly in the form of the concept of ecotravel in the latter document. In the former, STF emphasizes its long-term commitment to environmental organizations. STF's declarations begin with the following statement:

> In the following, the concept 'environment' refers to our total environment, that is nature, culture and the patterns of life connected with them. Our environment thus covers both our most unspoilt lands and the traditional cultural landscape and our population centres. (Svenska Turistföreningen 1990, p. 2, my translation)

STF asserts that we should strive to achieve rich and meaningful tourism which takes responsibility for the environment; among other things, it is vital to protect the identity of the various Swedish provinces, our traditions and patterns of life. Further, noise should not prevent us from being able to enjoy our leisure undisturbed. STF will implement its environmental programme by disseminating knowledge through publications, through the media and through measures at its facilities.

STF's policy programme notes initially that world tourism is undergoing a process of sweeping change, where demand and supply are increasingly being directed towards environmental experiences (Svenska Turistföreningen 1994). The policy programme for STF's internal activities is in accord with the WWF's commandments regarding the environmental adaptation of tourism, and ecotourism. For instance, STF states that it intends to work for environmentally adapted tourism throughout, that an environmental representative will be appointed in all its fields of activity and workplaces, that it will use locally produced goods, that it will provide good general and environmental information to the guest, encourage and inform people about public transport to the destination, and assess and control the quality of its activities from an environmental standpoint (Svenska Turistföreningen 1994, pp. 3–4).

CONCLUDING REMARKS AND COMMENTS

In the study the concept of sustainable tourism has been linked to development theory to provide a perspective on the content of the concept and the context to which it belongs. From the research standpoint, sustainable development has proved a difficult concept to handle because of its varying uses and meanings. One explanation of the different interpretations is that the concept is used in more or less radical contexts. An example of the difference in interpretation is its use in connection both with a functional top-down perspective on development issues and with the bottom-up development and territorially based perspective of self-reliance.

Furthermore, tourism has been placed in a social context since the tourism system can never function as an independent sub-system. The tourism system as such has been divided into its three basic components: the background factors of the tourists in the form of lifestyle, tourism and leisure travel and the impact of tourism on the destination. All these components contain aspects of sustainability. In the study it is primarily resource-based leisure tourism that has been studied and discussed.

The latter sections of Part I provide examples of what various organizations mean by and how they distinguish between the environmental adaptation of tourism and ecotourism, where the latter makes greater demands than the former. At the same time, it is claimed that all tourism should be adapted to the environment. Policy documents from the various organizations mainly reveal similarities. All of them indicate a desire to preserve natural and cultural environments in connection with the development of tourism. It may be noted that the general pattern is for environmental measures to be directed towards the destination. Certain of the organizations, e.g. Miljövårdsberedningen, and the document Agenda 21 for the travel and tourism industry, emphasize the preservation of the natural environment more than others. A further similarity is that all of them take up the issue of cooperation between various organizations and levels in society in order to solve the problems. Even the local adaptation of tourism and its usefulness are mentioned in most documents, but they are more clearly stated in certain of them, e.g. those from Australia. Perhaps this clarity results from the experience of conflict between different groups of people. The double nature of investing in the adaptation of tourism to the environment and ecotourism is clear. On the one hand, environmental measures are proposed and, on the other, there is an implicit intention that these measures should strengthen the competitiveness of products and countries. The commercial interest in conserving the resources on which the tourism industry is based implies that adapting tourism to the environment is a means of competition. A minority of the proposed measures concern the travel aspect of tourism and leisure. Where transport is considered at all, it is in summary terms. The exception is, to some extent, the Finnish Tourist Board, which discusses the question in clearer terms. I argue in this study that it is in transport that the greatest environment problems arise at the same time as they are, in some cases, more difficult to deal with.

PART 2

Lifestyle During Leisure

CHAPTER 3

Leisure

INTRODUCTION

This Part deals with lifestyle during leisure and its primary aim is to examine the activity and mobility patterns during leisure and tourist travel of Swedish people classified according to socio-economic, demographic and geographical characteristics. These patterns reveal aspects of people's lifestyle or, to put it in other words, they provide an indication of their lifestyle during leisure. Different groups of people choose different forms of travel, visit different places, travel to a varying extent. Our modes of travel and our lifestyle are, in their turn, related to our patterns of consumption. Our consumption of goods, services and travel affects demands for resources, the use of energy and waste disposal. It is then a question of sustainable development. In her survey Frändberg concludes that the lifestyle and consumer patterns of tourists 'generate much more waste than the life the residents live' (Frändberg 1993, p. 21).

How is a lifestyle formed? Generally speaking, a lifestyle is formed by the system of production and consumption in society. Certain needs are encouraged and trends established with the result that different activity and consumer patterns form parts of different lifestyles. The system of production and consumption can, however, be changed. In most of the countries in the rich world changes are taking place in the environmental field. The eco-labelling of goods and journeys which we see in the 1990s is very different from the 'throwaway' culture of the 1960s and 1970s and the lifestyles involved. It may also be noted that today adapting to the environment provides a competitive advantage in, for instance, the travel industry.

The main empirical material which will be used in this section is first a time-use survey conducted by Statistiska Centralbyrån (SCB) in 1990–91, in particular how different sections of the population use their leisure time. Second I make use of SCB's survey of living conditions, in particular, material on the Swedish population's holiday travel in 1991. This material provides information about how travel is distributed among different sections of the population and about which groups have a lifestyle that includes an active leisure-travel pattern.[13]

THE DEVELOPMENT OF LEISURE AND
THE CONCEPT OF LEISURE

Prior to the industrial revolution it was a small upper-class that had access to leisure in the sense of time over for other things than work. For most people at this time, the day consisted of work in order to survive. Industrialism created a working-class and the division of labour led to a different kind of workday for the majority of people. Men's time, above all, was divided between wage labour and leisure. For women the workday become a time of reproduction with responsibility for home and children. Free time was, then, a desirable but scarce good for the working-class and, at the beginning of the twentieth century, the trade union movement managed to gain acceptance for the demand for an eight-hour working day. Since the Second World War Swedish people have increased their leisure time through a shorter working week, longer holiday periods and a lower retirement age (SCB 1993). An increase in general welfare in the form of a higher material standard of living, the development of transport, and the expansion of the infrastructure has meant that leisure can in part be used for travelling. Leisure is important for society for several reasons, among them the fact that it gives people a chance to recover, and also that it provides valuable economic returns from the consumption of leisure articles and travel. In modern society leisure has become increasingly organized, which may be exemplified by the transition from children's unorganized play with a ball to football training organized by clubs. Tourism can be seen as a global project for organizing parts of leisure time into a development factor for the economy. The added value of tourism is here used productively (Lanfant and Graburn 1992, pp. 96–7).

The concept of leisure is multi-dimensional. Leisure is both the time when one is free from everyday duties, i.e. it is a kind of remainder when all the 'musts' have been done, and also a valuable dimension in the life of the individual, which can be filled with activities that broaden the mind. This reasoning implies that, given the right conditions, it is possible to choose freely what one wants to do during one's leisure time, from rest to demanding activities. However, even leisure is surrounded by restrictions which limit the scope for action, e.g. the time and money one has at one's disposal, the availability of transport, which is crucial for mobility, and the individual's own innate resources in the form of health or handicap. How leisure can be used is also related to factors such as phases in one's life-cycle, life mode and lifestyle (cf. Sandell 1995). Furthermore, leisure may also be seen as one way of demonstrating one's social status, e.g. making one's leisure visible and thereby letting it be a signal that one is wealthy (Veblen 1976).

One of the typical features of modern society is the division of functions with a high level of mobility between home, work, education, service and leisure activities. Many groups, e.g. households with children, experience that there is always a tight time schedule for their activities, which gives them the sense of never having enough time and thus causes stress (Schorr 1991). According to Hägerstrand (1984, pp. 7–19), our everyday life may be characterized as a 'cage of routine'. This perspective leads us to believe that we are prisoners in the present-day time–space structure that we have created for our lives. We often use the free time we have in the evenings, at weekends and during our holidays to try to change this state of affairs through, for instance, a change of environment or, if you will, a change of time–space. This is particularly true when we have longer connected periods of leisure. In limited periods like evenings, the spatial scope is also limited and we remain in the routinized everyday world.

How free is free time? Does a formal increase in leisure time really mean free time or do long journey times to various social activities mean that leisure time is really quite bound and structured? The part of our everyday life when we are not working is for most people a routinized time which is filled with transport to and from work and to services, with sleep, cooking and eating, personal care, child care, repairing the house, car, and so on. Really free time is thus quite limited, in particular for those who are working. We spend our free time in such activities as travel, sport, socializing and watching television.

Kelly (1983) claims that leisure is mainly determined on the basis of the relationship between the relative freedom people have to choose an activity and the informal rule system of the social context. The content of free time can be described in the following terms: on the one hand, leisure may have a large or small dimension of freedom and, on the other, it may take the form of a inner experience or it may have social significance. Kelly stresses the fact that leisure must be seen as part of the whole life situation and the conditions that this provides.

CONCEPTS FOR DESCRIBING SOCIAL DIFFERENCES

There are a number of concepts that relate to social differences between people, among them life mode, class and lifestyle. Definitions of life mode range from a narrow to a wide connotation and from being empirically oriented to being theoretically based. This suggests that there are several different directions in the analysis of life modes (Bäck-Wiklund and Lindfors 1974, 1990; Björnberg *et al.* 1980; Christensen and Højrup 1989; Højrup 1983; Jakobsson and Karlsson 1992). In most of these directions life mode refers to how people live their everyday lives and what type of social structure an individual can be placed in. Life mode analysis is, in general, oriented towards the study of the causes and consequences of social differences. However, the concept has different dimensions. One is that socio-economic conditions, including education, occupation and income, are crucial for how we live our lives. Another is a geographical dimension, whether we grew up or live and work in the country or the town. Further dimensions are gender and life-cycle. Life mode analysis can be seen as a development of class analysis.

> The analysis of class is based on ownership and exploitation relations in production. Classes are defined in relation to each other; so, for instance, a capitalist class is inconceivable without a working-class – and vice versa. There are at least three research orientations in class theory: one concerns the boundaries between classes and the size of the classes; a second, class consciousness, i.e. value structures in different classes; and a third, class actions, primarily in the form of conflict and struggle between classes. (Jakobsson and Karlsson 1992, pp. 7–8, my translation)

If life mode analysis has its background in the analysis of class, then lifestyle analysis may be defined as an offshoot of the concept of life mode. The task of lifestyle analysis is to determine and reveal the content of different ways of living. Practising one's lifestyle means carrying out activities which reveal value patterns, e.g. the group one belongs to. Examples of lifestyle categories are people whose orientation is towards work, family, fellowship or consumption (Bjurström 1990–91).

Theories on social differences can be related to time-geography in the sense that access to and the utilization of time and space depend on the social group one lives in. Theories on social differences also complement time-geography by revealing the 'invisible' structures which make up different sub-cultures. Time-geography can, in its turn, be used to demonstrate empirically patterns of activity in life modes and lifestyles.

GENERAL COMMENTS ON THE TIME-USE STUDY 1990–91

Introduction

From September 1990 to May 1991 Statistiska Centralbyrån conducted a survey of the way the Swedish population between the ages of 20 and 64 made use of their time. The data were collected with the aid of time diaries during two 24-hour periods selected at random. Christmas week and Easter week were excluded from the selection. The respondents noted their activities in their own words in their diaries and the activities were then coded by SCB. The minimum time limit for an activity to be noted was ten minutes. The total sample consisted of 3943 people and the non-response rate was 25 per cent, which means that 3400 people kept a diary of what they did during one weekday and one 24-hour period during a weekend.[14] The main groups of activities coded from the diaries are:

- Gainful employment. This refers to the working-life sphere or paid labour. A gross working-hours concept is used, which includes all time set aside for work, e.g. journeys to and from work. Even spare-time jobs are included. Note that this use of the concept of working-hours differs from that used in other public statistics.
- Work in the home. This refers to the private sphere or unpaid labour and covers most of the jobs involved in looking after the home and family: housework, repairs, care of the children and shopping.
- Education. This refers to all the activities connected with studies.
- Personal needs. This includes time for physiological needs such as sleeping, eating and attending to one's personal hygiene.
- Free time. Free time in the survey is a remainder category, i.e. it includes the activities left over after all the other categories have been classified. Free time is dominated by what are usually termed leisure activities, e.g. sports and outdoor activities, clubs and societies, entertainment and culture, socializing, reading and watching television.

In the present study the focus is on the use of time for free-time activities. In this context, it should be remembered that leisure activities are only part of a whole. It should also be noted that the figures given are averages for whole sections of the population and that it may be the case that no one individual has divided his or her time in exactly the manner indicated. The time-use study as a whole is not specially adapted to studies of the use of leisure time. First, the summer holiday period is not included in the survey nor are, as we said, the Christmas and Easter weeks. This means, for instance, that the most important periods for long-distance tourism and leisure travel are not included in the material. Second, the survey is limited to those who are gainfully employed, which excludes both young people and old-age pensioners. These are the groups that from a life-cycle perspective have a greater amount of free time at their disposal than, for instance, families with small children. These limitations in the survey thus mean that there are shortcomings in an analysis of leisure time. Despite these objections, the material provides a good basis for illustrating leisure on weekdays and at weekends. The longer and more temporary leisure travel will be dealt with later using other material.

The Structure of the Use of Time

The overarching structure of the use of time by the Swedish population is given in Table 3.1. As is seen, 36% or more than 60 of the week's 168 hours are used for some form of work. On average about 20% of the time is free time. Free time represents about 17% of weekdays and almost 30% of the use of time at weekends. Less than one hour per week has been impossible to classify.

Table 3.1. The overarching structure of the use of time by Swedish people (aged 20–64) in 1990/91. *Source*: Rydenstam (1992, pp. 24–6).

Main activity	Time spent per week hours and minutes	Time spent per week percentage
Gainful employment	34 hrs 15 min	20
Work in the home	26 hrs 40 min	16
Education	2 hrs 5 min	1
Personal needs	70 hrs 30 min	42
Free time	34 hrs 0 min	20
Other		<1
Total	168 hrs	100

The Structure of the Use of Time by Sex and Age Group

The differences in the use of time between the sexes seen over the whole week and for all work are small, taken overall (Rydenstam 1992, p. 29). One difference is that men are gainfully employed to a greater extent and that women spend more of their time on work in the home. Furthermore, there is a difference between age groups. The 35–49 age group spend more time at work than the others.

The two large time-use categories which remain after work are personal needs and free time. The material shows that men overall have somewhat more free time and that women spend somewhat more time on personal needs. The age group that overall has least free time is the 35–49 group. Those with most free time are in the 50–64 group.

Regional Differences in the Use of Time

The figures show that the regional differences overall and separately for each homogeneity region (or functional region – H-region) and each main category of activity are very small (Rydenstam 1992, p. 42).[15] The differences in use of time as a whole between the big city, Stockholm, and the northern rural area are thus negligible.

HOW IS FREE TIME USED?

The Overall Use of Leisure Time

Women had almost 33 hours per week free time and men just over 35 hours per week. An overview of the use of time for the various categories of activity is given below.

- Sports and outdoor activities. Seven per cent or two and a half hours per week is devoted on average to this activity. Men spend one hour more than women. According to Rydenstam (1992, p. 67), it is possibly the case that women walk to a greater extent than men, who spend more time on sport and exercise.
- Clubs and societies account for 1.5% of the free time per week on average.
- Entertainment and culture take up less than 1% of the free time per week. Entertainment and culture, and club activities are the activities on which least time is spent, altogether less than one hour per week.
- Social activities take up 22% of the free time or just under eight hours per week, more for women, eight and a half hours, and somewhat less for men, just over seven hours. Visits from or to relatives and friends account for less than 6% of the free time, which is just over two hours per week (4% of the free time is spent on visits to relatives and friends and just under 2% on visits from relatives and friends). Telephone calls take up almost 4% of the free time or about one and a half hours per week.
- Television and radio. Watching television, including video films, is the predominant leisure activity. Over 33% of the free time is spent in this way: 37% for men or almost 13 hours per week and over 30% for women or 10 hours and 15 minutes per week. Listening to the radio is, however, not as common, with just over half an hour a week devoted to it.[16]
- Reading occupies 12% of the free time or altogether four hours per week.

- Hobbies take up just over 4% of the free time or one hour and 45 minutes per week.
- Travel in connection with free time accounts for over 7% of the free time, which means about two and a half hours per week (Rydenstam 1992, pp. 68–9).

A Life-Cycle and Gender Perspective on Free Time

Generally speaking, an individual has a great deal of free time during his or her youth. This free time is somewhat reduced when someone marries and settles down and is considerably reduced for families with children. As the children grow up, free time increases. If we specifically consider the travel category, we find that it accounts for the greatest proportion of free time for those without children, young people and the middle-aged up to 44. There is a tendency in most of these groups for men to travel more than women. There is a difference between men's and women's free time in that women's free time is divided into more and shorter episodes than men's. This is probably explained by the fact that women are responsible for work in the home where a job must be done when the need arises. This is true both on weekdays and at weekends (Rydenstam 1992, p. 73).

Where the Respondents Were during their Free Time on the Day of the Survey

The respondents were asked to indicate in the time diaries where they were and what movements they made on the day of the survey. The clearly predominant place, measured in time, proved to be in or near the home, which means 69 of the free time or more than 21 hours per week. Women spent somewhat more time in the home or close to it than men. Respondents spent altogether 1% of their free time in or near their weekend cottage, mainly at the weekend. An average of 12% of the free time during the week was spent in other people's homes (Rydenstam 1992, p. 98).

The Use of Transport for Journeys during Free Time

The car is used for 60% of the travel time for journeys during free time. Men use it to a somewhat greater extent than women. Public transport is used for 16% for the travel time; 14% of the journeys are made on foot and 3% by cycle. Women walk more than men but otherwise the differences are small (Rydenstam 1992, p. 101).

Perceived Lack of Time (Stress)

Apart from the time diaries, the survey asked a number of questions to complement the picture of how time is used. Some of them concerned the feeling of not having enough time:

Do you usually have so much to do on weekdays that you have difficulty in getting everything done?

Are there things that you would like to do on an ordinary weekday but cannot because of lack of time?

If you answer yes to the last question:

If you had more time during the week what would you mainly spend it doing? (Rydenstam 1992, p. 103, my translation)

The material has previously shown that certain groups, e.g. parents with small children, have less free time at their disposal than other groups. It is interesting to see whether the above questions can provide more information about the lack of time. The third question is intended to classify the lack of time people experience.

Altogether, 55% say they do not have enough time on weekdays. There is no difference between men and women in this respect. From a life-cycle perspective, it is the parents of small children who indicate the greatest lack of time. About 70% of two-parent families and single mothers, both with small children, indicate that they do not have enough time. What is important for these groups is to have more time for domestic work and time for the children. It is only in these groups that there is a conflict about how they would like to use this extra time. In all the other groups there is a desire for more time for leisure activities. The study shows that over 30% of the total population would like to have more time for leisure activities on weekdays (Rydenstam 1992, p. 105).

CONCLUDING REMARKS ON LIFESTYLE AND SUSTAINABILITY DURING LEISURE

The material that has been presented has its shortcomings in revealing how leisure time is used, in particular for long-distance leisure travel. Tourism and long-distance leisure travel will be discussed on the basis of other data in the next chapter. Even the mobility aspect of people's lifestyle during leisure will be considered later. The data presented here do, however, provide a fairly balanced picture of the activities of present-day Swedes during their leisure time, which, in its turn, gives some indication of lifestyle.

A selection of items from the report indicates some of the typical leisure activities of the Swedes. The predominant leisure activities at home are watching television, being together with friends and family, and reading. The predominant leisure activities outside the home are sports, outdoor pastimes and travel, where the private car is the dominant form of transport. Those without children, young people and the middle-aged up to 44 spend the greatest proportion of their leisure in travel. Men tend to travel somewhat more frequently than women during their leisure time, where the private car is the primary form of transport for men. Generally speaking, we have a lot of free time at our disposal when we are young, and least free time when we have small children. Further, the majority of people, it is shown, live a stressful life, which to some extent is a result of the division of functions in society into a series of activities located in different places. One aspect of the present-day sense of being pressed for time concerns the sustainability of civil society. It may be asked whether civil society would not function more harmoniously than at present if we could integrate functions more and thus reduce the pressure. Naturally, this is not the only reason for the lack of time; the material shows, for instance, that it is parents with small children who, because of their situation, are most exposed to stress.

CHAPTER 4

Tourism

INTRODUCTION

In general it may be said that the countries in the rich world have seen an enormous growth in the opportunities for leisure travel since the end of the Second World War. The reasons for this are primarily the increase in leisure time and a consequent shortening of working hours, a better economic and material standard of living, the explosive development of motoring and charter flights, and improvements in the infrastructure in society. Furthermore, the growing demand for leisure activities has led to a huge increase in all types of leisure articles and tourism products and in the infrastructure for leisure and tourism. Travel, especially during free time, was once the prerogative of the few but the developments outlined above led to the emergence of mass tourism in the late 1950s. This form of tourism, which is typified by the charter flight, has grown exponentially. However, a new tendency became noticeable in the 1980s. A comparison of Swedes' leisure travel in 1978 and 1994 carried out by Frändberg shows that package tours have decreased from 83% in 1978 to 56% in 1994 (Frändberg 1996, p. 29). This would suggest that a change is taking place in the geographical pattern of tourism from traditional mass tourism to the late modern society's differentiated travel pattern in smaller groups (cf. Nash 1992, p. 219).

The main feature of mass tourism is the very large volume of visitors concentrated in one place. Further, the tours are often standardized. The primary destinations were and are resorts by the sea and in the mountains with good sun and snow conditions, and big cities. It is people in the rich world who are by far the greatest travellers, either within their own cultural sphere or to the developing world. The driving forces behind mass tourism are said to be the desire to get away from everyday life and the search for the four Ss: 'sun, sea, sand and sex' or 'sun, ski, snow and sex' (Smith and Eadington 1992, p. 6). Naturally, further key words may be added, but the symbolism of these four is probably sufficient to characterize the underlying motives. The consequences of mass tourism have been described by Smith and Eadington in the following manner.

> For the locals – the hosts – the concerns may be of promises unfulfilled, destruction of an older and simpler way of life, inadequacy of employment opportunities, or dissatisfaction with other economic changes which came with tourism development. For tourists the view is often summarized with statements such as 'this used to be a nice place, but now it is ruined' because of overcrowding, overcommercialization, or overdevelopment. (Smith and Eadington 1992, p. 8)

The main volume of tourism travel today still consists of mass tourists, but during the 1980s, as we have noted, new and more specialized forms of travel began to emerge in the tourism arena, such as ecotourism, adventure and wilderness tourism. What is typical of most of these forms of tourism is that they focus on nature. During the 1990s, the corresponding differentiation has reached culture tourism. Here we find, for instance, a revival in educational travel, a form of travel which is sometimes said to be the origin of modern tourism (Karlsson 1994). Typical of these specialized forms of travel is that the groups are small and there is a well-defined objective where nature and culture form the basic conditions for the journey. These changes can at least in part be seen as a shift in lifestyle (cf. Horn *et al.* 1995; MacCanell 1989, 1992).

Another noticeable tendency in late modern society is that leisure activities are being devised which are concentrated in time and have shorter planning and follow-up times (Horn *et al.* 1995, pp. 83–9; Schorr 1991). The stressful everyday lifestyle of modern man is thus reflected in tourism and leisure activities. The motivation in tourism and leisure activities seems in many cases to be the search for particular experiences rather than for specific places (cf. Sandell 1995). This reasoning is valid for mass tourism as well as for the extra-ordinary experiences of alternative tourism, e.g. in the form of mountain-biking in the mountains or bungy jumping.

There is an extensive flora of terms in the literature for both mass tourism and alternative specialized forms of tourism. Moreover, the concepts are seldom well defined. Mass tourism is sometimes designated as 'hard tourism', 'commercial/conventional', 'large-scale', 'capitalistic', or 'foreign-owned' (Pearce, D. 1992, p. 19). The corresponding terms used for alternative tourism are: 'soft tourism', 'small-scale tourism', 'green tourism', 'ecotourism' and 'sustainable tourism'. A brief survey of articles in scientific journals in recent years suggests that the term 'sustainable tourism', with a global and holistic perspective, and the term 'ecotourism', which is limited to a special form of travel, seem to dominate the debate and studies.[17] Further, the local perspective is emphasized in ecotourism and this distinguishes it from sustainable tourism development, which has both a global and a local perspective. Moreover, sustainable tourism development is a process as distinct from ecotourism and other alternative forms of tourism, which are more a matter of developing limited projects.

As regards trends, the 1990s have become the decade of ecotourism, primarily as a result of the growing awareness of the negative impact of mass tourism (Laarman and Perdue 1989; Place 1991; Smith and Eadington 1992, p. 5; Weaver 1991; Widstrand 1993; Wilkinson 1989). Is ecotourism a form of sustainable tourism? Serious ecotourism seems to be an excellent form of sustainable tourism. The product is, in many cases, well adapted both to the local community and to the environment. One problem with long-distance travel is the high consumption of energy per person and the emissions that it entails. However, where ecotourism travel is concerned, this must be weighed against the fact that the volume of travel in mass tourism is considerably greater and that mass tourism in general entails a high degree of exploitation of a place, which often has various kinds of negative impacts. Even tourism which is classed as ecotourism may have serious consequences if the environment in the area is extremely sensitive (e.g. Hall, M. 1992). A further problem with ecotourism is that it might lead to a previously unexploited area being developed for mass tourism. The time aspect is important here. In the short term ecotourism may seem attractive but what is the long-term impact on areas that are used for this purpose?

LIFESTYLES, TOURIST TYPOLOGIES AND SUSTAINABILITY

In tourism research there are a number of classifications and typologies of tourists relating, for instance, to motives for the journey, attitudes, behaviour, activities, needs, demand and consumer patterns (cf. Gunn 1988, pp. 100–1; Lowyck et al. 1992; Murphy 1985, pp. 5–7). Poon discusses the differences in values, expectations and behaviour between the new differentiated and specialized forms of tourism and conventional tourism (Poon in Burns and Holden 1995, p. 223). These differences are presented in Table 4.1. Even if the types of tourist indicated in the list are stereotypes, it is still interesting in that it reveals a change of attitude among tourists.

Andersson and Ramqvist (1997) studied what had happened to Swedish tourism from the 1950s to the mid 1990s. They found that the following major changes had occurred:

Table 4.1. Differences between conventional tourism and new specialized tourism. Source: Poon (1993).

Old tourists	New tourists
Search for the sun	Experience something new
Follow the masses	Want to be in charge
Here today, gone tomorrow	See and enjoy but do not destroy
Show that you have been	Just for the fun of it
Having	Being
Superiority	Understanding
Like attractions	Like sport and nature
Cautious	Adventurous
Eat in the hotel dining room	Try out local fare
Homogeneous	Hybrid

- From uniformity to diversity. The supply of tourism products and travel alternatives has increased and there are more categories of tourists today than previously. This corresponds to the general development of society in Sweden from an incipient welfare state in the 1950s to a late modern, capitalist consumer society in the 1990s.
- From ignorance to greater knowledge. Tourists today seem to have a much greater knowledge of the world and better general knowledge of languages and other cultures. This can be partly explained by the huge developments in education and the media.
- From relaxation to activity. The material indicates that previously tourists often used to go away to relax and visit relatives and friends whilst today they are much more interested in activities.
- From family travel to individual travel. Here the material suggests that previously journeys were often made together with the family whilst today people tend to travel individually or in small groups.

Svalastog (1985, pp. 7–11, 1994, pp. 100–8) has further developed Aubert's (1969, pp. 113–40) sociological tourist typologies and related the demand that these create to the activities and facilities which they use and the energy consumption, pollution and costs that accompany them. The typologies show the resources that each category of tourist requires from the local community. They are closely related to lifestyle in that they are, in the main, based on the attitudes and/or behaviour of tourists.

- The wilderness tourist. This tourist wishes to get away from the social control of his or her own society and does not want to be received by a host society. He or she wants to get close to nature and to learn more about himself or herself. Wilderness tourists are not a large group and there are seldom many of them in one place at one time. Examples of activities which meet their needs are hiking, mountaineering, ocean sailing, diving. Natural resources are crucial. Possible demands from this group of tourists include continuous unspoilt areas, clean water, good hunting grounds, and fishing waters and an intact flora and fauna. In general, the areas that are used are sensitive. One problem, however, lies in developing a saleable product. Svalastog describes the problems of energy consumption, pollution and the related costs in the following terms:

  > The holiday trip (expedition) is extremely demanding in terms of energy, and costly if the whole project is taken into account, including equipment, the long journey (West Europeans and Americans) to, for instance, Nepal in Asia, trips arranged by the Norwegian Tourist Association to Kilimanjaro in Africa, trips to the South Pole, which are being planned by the Swedish Tourist Association, skiing expeditions to Nustagh Ata in Asia (China) or the classic ocean races such as Whitbread Round the World Race. (Svalastog 1994, p. 102, my translation)

- The antitourist. This tourist does not want to be considered a tourist but prefers to be part of the normal social activities of the community he or she is visiting. The typical antitourist visits friends and relatives, i.e. network-based travel. Examples of suitable activities and facilities include a holiday home in the tourist's former home district, farm holidays, private accommodation, cabins and boarding houses. The group is relatively impervious to marketing.

  > This form of tourism requires small resources, because the tourists are stationary and because the form demands little from the receiving area. In the main, existing buildings are used, and the antitourist adopts the local standard as regards food, drink and entertainment. (Svalastog 1994, pp. 101–2, my translation)

- The emigrant tourist. This tourist wishes to get away from his or her homeland for political reasons, tax reasons etc. or wishes to live in a better climate. There are two subgroups here. The first already have the necessary economic resources and do not need to work in the country visited. The second subgroup is the drifter category, who live simply and take temporary jobs to support themselves. The emigrant tourist lives a largely everyday life in the community he or she visits, which makes this form different from most other tourist typologies.

> The emigrant tourist remains in the same place over long periods and, typically, lives simply. A stationary existence and sober lifestyle result in low energy consumption. (Svalastog 1994, p. 103, my translation)

- The sightseeing tourist. This tourist, who has great spending power, wishes to see the world in a fast and comfortable manner. Typical of this group is that they 'pick places', which means that they have a subject of conversation, photographs etc. for later use in a social context at home. Examples of activities that meet the needs of this group include bus trips along typical sightseeing routes with room and board in good quality hotels, ocean cruises and well organized tours. This type of tourist is interested in both natural resources, i.e. they seek beautiful landscapes (at least as a setting) and synthetic sights. Svalastog describes the group's energy consumption, pollution and costs in the following terms:

  > The daily consumption of the sightseeing tourist on a conducted tour has traditionally been very high and in the group we find much
  >
  > – demonstrative leisure (one cruise after another).
  >
  > – demonstrative consumption (traditionally such expensive holiday forms that only the wealthy or otherwise privileged members of a society can afford them. Compare here those who have formed the main body of this group in Eastern Europe).
  >
  > – demonstrative leisure skills. That is insight into social customs, standards and activities. In this group material consumption is high both in the home and in the tourist situation. (Svalastog 1994, p. 104, my translation)

- The knowledge seeker or the connoisseur. This tourist wants to learn about the host society and experience its culture. Often it is a question of the same interests as the individual has at home, e.g. in such fields as archaeology, animal life and social conditions. The group typically consists of people with a good economy and a good level of education. Tourists in this group may, on the one hand, select high-class cultural arrangements or, on the other, seek natural phenomena such as photo safaris and certain forms of hunting and fishing.

  > The connoisseur travels often and long distances just to stay for a short time. The many and long journeys demand a great deal of energy, and daily consumption is, in general, often high. As a collector, he or she is often cynical in purchasing, plundering and illegally exporting antiquities, animals and plants. (Svalastog 1994, p. 105, my translation)

- The sun and snow worshipper. Sometimes the tourist seeks pleasure and well-being in an area with plenty of sun and a good climate, in other cases, in a specially prepared winter landscape. The host community is looked upon as relatively uninteresting. Charter tourism to the Mediterranean area and tourism to winter sports resorts are examples of this form of tourism. The product is based on natural and cultural resources which have been specially prepared and standardized. The tourist adopts a non-everyday role.

    The sun tourist is a mass phenomenon. This is, above all, a holiday form for the masses. It requires small energy resources as regards destination and transport. Daily consumption is moderately high. (Svalastog 1994, p. 106, my translation)

- The activity tourist. Svalastog has assigned Aubert's original typology to this group and the following one. The tourist typology may be oriented towards both summer and/or winter activities and one of the objectives is that the activities should provide physical exercise in line with the individual's capacity. The tourist makes some demands on the natural and cultural resources but they are not particularly great, which means in general that he or she does not damage the resources. In this respect, the typology is the opposite of the wilderness tourist. However, the tourist does place demands on the facilities. Examples of suitable activities are winter sports facilities of little to average difficulty or water activities such as sailing and surfing.

    The activity tourist is a tourist who remains in one place. This form of holiday does not demand much equipment so the daily costs are low to medium. The energy requirements are also moderate. (Svalastog 1994, p. 107, my translation)

- The utility tourist. This tourist wants to use his or her leisure to pick berries, gather mushrooms, fish and hunt. The whole family is often involved and, usually, they live simply. This form of tourism is based on natural resources and is, in general, unproblematic for local natural and cultural conditions. The product may consist of offering equipment for such activities as fishing.

    This is also a form where the tourist remains in one place. Daily consumption is low. Functionally, much of the everyday sphere is introduced into the holiday sphere. (Svalastog 1994, p. 107, my translation)

Some of these tourist typologies are primarily based on good natural conditions. These are the wilderness tourist, the sun and snow worshipper and the utility tourist. The typologies that are mainly oriented towards cultural conditions are the emigrant tourist and, even more so, the knowledge seeker or connoisseur. The main type that seeks synthetic tourist attractions is the activity tourist. The sightseeing tourist has a social motive as the driving force behind his or her journey. The antitourist represents a category that is not commercially oriented. The categories whose adaptation to the environment Svalastog most questions are: the wilderness tourist, the sightseeing tourist and the knowledge seeker or connoisseur. This is interesting since the new and specialized forms of tourism, in this case ecotourism and wilderness tourism as well as educational travel, can be assigned to these energy- and resource-intensive forms and are thus questionable from a sustainable standpoint.

In the context of this study, the tourist typologies presented here should be seen as an example of a theoretical discussion of the environmental impacts of tourist typologies. Given the scope of the study, it has not been possible to test the typologies empirically.

SWEDES' TOURISM TRAVEL

This section provides the details of why, where and how Swedish people make tourist trips (Turistdelegationen 1997). The information refers to domestic and foreign travel in 1996 and includes journeys with overnight stays. The percentages indicate the proportion for each of the categories of the total amount of travel. The information is mainly drawn from the Tourism and Travel Database (TDB).

Frändberg also presents current details about Swedes' domestic and foreign tourism travel (Frändberg 1996). In this case the information comes from the survey of travel habits conducted by Statistiska Centralbyrån in 1994. Frändberg's aim was to study the use of resources and the impact on the environment of Swedes' tourism travel. To achieve this goal, Frändberg processed the above mentioned survey of travel habits and also made a number of comparisons with a similar study from 1978. The results she presents from these surveys concern the mobility patterns of Swedes in connection with long-distance travel and, in particular, tourism travel. Further, the distribution of tourism travel in the population is classified according to age, sex and income.

In Table 4.4 travel has been broadly classified as leisure, journeys in connection with the reproductive needs of the household, i.e. service, or journeys in connection with work. In its turn, leisure travel has been divided in three sub-categories: journeys to visit relatives and friends, journeys to a weekend cottage and tourism journeys.

Table 4.2. Swedes' domestic leisure journeys in 1996.

The primary aims of the journeys were:

• To meet relatives and friends	46.4%
• To go to their holiday cottage	16.4%
• Sunbathing and seaside holidays	3.9%
• Skiing	3.7%
• Relaxation	3.5%
• Other	26.1%
Total	100 %

The primary destinations were:

• The city and province of Stockholm	14.6%
• The province of Göteborg and Bohuslän	11.3%
• The province of Dalarna	7.8%
• The city and province of Malmö	5.2%
• The province of Jämtland	4.5%
• The province of Östergötland	4.3%
• Other	52.3%
Total	100 %

The transport used was:

• Private car	78%
• Train	9%
• Bus	6%
• Plane	3%
• Other	4%
Total	100%

Finally, the following forms of accommodation, measured in overnight stays, were the most frequently used:[18]

• Living with relatives and friends	about	60,000,000	42%
• Own cottage or holiday apartment	about	40,000,000	28%
• Rented cabin or apartment	about	15,000,000	10%
• Hotels		14,679,000	10%
• Camping sites		10,113,000	7%
• Cabin villages		3,215,000	2%
• Youth hostels		867,000	<1%
Total		143,874,000	

Table 4.3. Swedes' foreign leisure journeys in 1996.

The primary aims of the journeys were:

• To meet relatives and friends	26.2%
• Sunbathing and seaside holidays	14.8%
• Pleasure and entertainment	8.0%
• Relaxation	7.3%
• Sightseeing	4.0%
• Visiting big cities	3.7%
• Other	36%
Total	100%

The primary destinations were:

• Denmark	16.1%
• Finland including Åland	12.6%
• Norway	10.6%
• Spain including the Canaries	9.9%
• Greece	8.8%
• Germany	7.1%
• Other	34.9%
Total	100%

The transport used was:

• Plane	46%
• Private car	31%
• Ferry	9%
• Bus	8%
• Train	4%
• Other	2%
Total	100%

Table 4.4. Number and percentage of domestic and foreign long-distance journeys (over 100 km one way) by purpose, 1994. *Source*: Frändberg (1996, p. 22).

Object of journey	Domestic travel		Foreign travel		Total	
	no. in millions	%	no. in millions	%	no. in millions	%
Leisure, of this:						
Visits to relatives/friends	13.7	25	0.9	12	14.5	23
Weekend cottage	6.8	12	0.4	6	7.2	12
Tourism	15.0	27	3.9	56	18.9	30
Service	2.0	4	0.1	1	2.1	3
Work	13.7	25	1.6	23	15.3	25
Other/no information	4.2	8	0.1	2	4.3	7
Total	55.3	100	7.0	100	62.3	100

Tourism journeys are the largest single category of long-distance journeys and it is the clearly dominant category of foreign journeys. Tourism accounted for 15 per cent of the Swedish population's total mobility in 1994 and tourism travel for 21.7 billion person-kilometres of the long-distance journeys in 1994, which may be compared with the Swedish population's journeys between home and work, which in the same year accounted for 21.8 billion person-kilometres (Frändberg 1996, p. 23). As Frändberg points out, the comparison is interesting since journeys to work by car have been the focus of political discussion on transport and its environmental impact, whilst tourism journeys, which are at the same level, have received little consideration (*ibid.*, pp. 23–4). The various types of journey have different temporal patterns during the year. Leisure travel shows a distinct peak during the summer months, July in particular, whilst journeys involving work, business and service show a similarly distinct decline in July but otherwise maintain an even level throughout the rest of the year (Sveriges Nationalatlas 1992, pp. 40–1).

According to Krantz and Vilhelmson (1996, p. 33), the total amount of leisure travel, measured in person-kilometres, decreased between 1978 and 1996 from 46% to 40%. A comparison between the sub-categories of long-distance domestic leisure travel in 1978 and 1996 shows that visits to relatives and friends decreased from about 47% to about 39%. Even travel to weekend cottages decreased over the same period from about 22% to about 19%. On the other hand, tourism journeys increased their share from about 32% to about 43% (Frändberg 1996, p. 25).

Frändberg's figures correspond to the figures from the tourism database presented earlier regarding the purpose of the journeys, and under this heading it is the two categories, visiting relatives and friends and travelling to one's weekend cottage, that are comparable. The differences between the figures are considerable as regards visits to relatives and friends, where the percentages given in the tourism database are almost twice as large as the figures in the survey of travel habits. The explanation for this probably lies in the construction of the questions and in the fact that there is a difference between the two surveys as regards the classification of purpose.

The figures given above indicate why, where and how the Swedes travel as tourists. However, they tell us nothing about the distribution of travel among different sections of the population and thereby which groups of people have a lifestyle that includes an active leisure travel pattern. The latest available material indicating the travel patterns of different sections of the population are the surveys on the living conditions of Swedes by Statistiska Centralbyrån and Frändberg's presentation of SCB's surveys of travel habits.

TOURISM TRAVEL FOR DIFFERENT SECTIONS OF THE POPULATION IN SWEDEN

Introduction

Statistiska Centralbyrån conducts continuous surveys of the living conditions of the Swedish population. Normally it is the 16 to 84 age groups who are studied. The data are mainly collected by means of personal interviews with a sample of the population. Various areas of welfare are studied in turn year by year. The report 'Fritid 1976–91' (Leisure 1976–91) (SCB 1993) provides information about the following areas of activity: outdoor life, sport and exercise, cultural activities, entertainment and hobbies, club activities, holiday trips and access to weekend cottage, and the leisure situation for children aged 7–15. The results presented here are primarily drawn from the 1990–91 survey but comparisons are also made with the 1978 and 1982–83 surveys.

General Information about Swedes' Holiday Travel

Over a twelve-month period about 2.2 million men (66%) and 2.3 million women (69%) in Sweden between the ages of 16 and 84 make a holiday or pleasure trip lasting at least a week. Holiday travel is more common among the younger age groups, 16–44, where about 75% made such a trip. The corresponding figures for the 45–64 age group is about 72% and for the 65–74 age group just over 50%.

Finally, about 35% of the 75–84 age group make a holiday trip or rather a pleasure trip since the last two groups are pensioners. Furthermore, the younger age groups are away on holiday for a longer period than the older ones (SCB 1993, pp. 105–9). Altogether 2.8 million men and women aged 16–84, or 43%, make a holiday or pleasure trip abroad lasting at least a week during a twelve-month period. Journeys abroad are also more common among the younger age groups, in particular young women, than among older groups.

According to the figures from the 1994 survey of travel habits as processed by Frändberg (1996, p. 31), tourism travel is relatively evenly distributed across different age categories of the Swedish population. There is, however, a clear dividing line in that people under the age of 55 travel more as tourists than older people do. Frändberg has also looked at which groups account for the 10% longest journeys and the results show that there is a degree of concentration to those aged 25–44. Frändberg (1996, p. 33) indicates that, on the whole, men make more long-distance journeys than women, 57% to 43%. Broken down into subgroups, the results show that men make more journeys long-distance on business and women to visit relatives and friends. As concerns tourism travel, there is no difference between the sexes, as regards either frequency or distance. On studying the 10% who travel farthest, we find, however, that women dominate by 55% to 45% for men. As is apparent from the presentation, men's more work-related long-distance travel can be seen as a substitute for other long-distance leisure travel.

The results from the two surveys referred to do not differ significantly as regards age and sex. Taken together, the surveys give a more balanced picture of the differences in long-distance travel that have been mentioned.

Social Differences in Holiday Travel

There are considerable differences in holiday travel between different socio-economic groups (SCB 1993, pp. 109–12). Eighty-five per cent of senior salaried staff make a holiday trip. Holiday travel decreases in the 'lower' socio-economic groups and among the early retired and unemployed it is 55%. Further, salaried staff are away for a longer period than workers. Other groups who are not away on holiday as much as salaried staff are farmers (33%) and single parents (65%).

Frändberg (1996 p. 34) also indicates that her study of figures from the 1994 survey of travel habits shows that people with higher incomes travel more on tourist trips than those with lower incomes. On the other hand, income does not seem to play any role in long-distance journeys to relatives and friends.

Regional Differences in Holiday Travel

There are even regional differences in holiday travel. It is much more common for people living in the Stockholm area (H-region 1, 80%) to make holiday journeys than for those living in the northern rural area (H-region 6, about 50%). Moreover, those who live in the Stockholm area are, on average, away for a much longer period than those living in the northern rural area. Big city dwellers also travel on longer foreign holidays to a greater extent than those living in rural areas (SCB 1993, p. 110).

Differences in Holiday Accommodation

It is possible to see the choice of holiday accommodation as at least in part a lifestyle phenomenon. If we consider camping, i.e. those living in a tent or caravan/mobile home, we find that they are primarily younger people and people living together rather than single people. Further, it is more common among workers than among salaried staff and more common among those living in smaller places in the country than among big city dwellers (SCB 1993, pp. 113–14).

The Development of Tourism Travel in Sweden

The trend in holiday travel in Sweden in the 16–84 age groups over the period 1976–91, i.e. those who made a holiday trip lasting at least a week, showed a relatively moderate increase of 6% (1976: 61%, 1982–83: 63%, 1991: 67%). Women's holiday travel increased somewhat more than men's in the period 1976–83. Thereafter the trend was reversed. The group which showed the overall largest increase in 1982–91, from 60% to 69%, were those aged 45–64. From a life-cycle perspective this change may be seen as a generation shift where a younger generation that is used to travelling continues the habit as they grow older. Foreign holiday travel decreased from 47% to 45% over the same period. For men the proportion of foreign holidays decreased from 47% to 44%, whilst women remained at an unchanged level, 46%, which can be related to the fact that women became more economically and socially independent during the 1980s. One of the main factors behind the decrease in foreign travel was probably the economic depression in Sweden with a weak currency as a result. There are clear differences between the socio-economic groups regarding those who make a holiday trip at all. Seventy-four per cent of salaried staff made a foreign trip in 1976 and 77% in 1990–91. The figure for blue-collar workers remained in the region of 57% throughout the period. The differences between the groups as regards foreign holiday travel increased in 1982–91. The proportion of unskilled workers taking a foreign holiday decreased, whilst salaried staff increased their foreign travel during the period. This probably reflects greater differences in

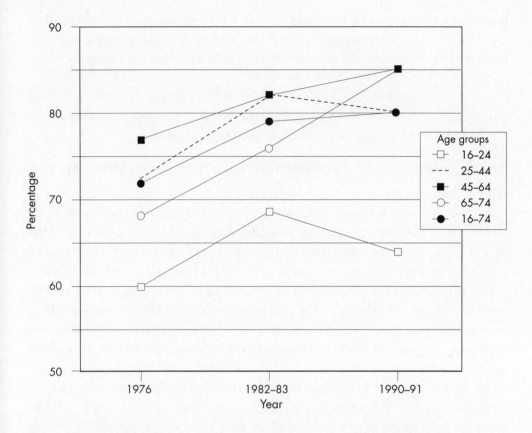

Figure 4.1. The percentage of the population in various age groups who, at least once a week, worked in the garden, walked in the countryside, walked for pleasure/exercise, went fishing, or made trips in their own boat in 1976, 1982–83 and 1990–91. *Source*: SCB (1993, p. 66)

income between socio-economic groups in the 1980s. The regional differences in the total holiday travel over the period 1976–91 show that those living in the Stockholm region remained at an unchanged level, whilst the corresponding figures for the regions tended to show an increase. As regards foreign travel, there was a decrease in the northern rural areas from 33% to 26%, whilst the levels were relatively unchanged in the other H-regions (SCB 1993, pp. 114–16).

Frändberg's comparison of the frequency of all long-distance journeys between 1978 and 1994 shows that travel was more concentrated to the younger age groups, those aged 15–34, in 1978 than 1994. One explanation for this might be that the economic climate was tougher in 1994 than in 1978. Frändberg and the survey of travel habits indicate that tourist travel increased between 1978 and 1994. Moreover, there was a more even distribution between the various age groups in 1994 than in 1978. This can be seen as an expression of the fact that the 'first tourism generation' continued their intensive travelling at the same time as the younger generation also adopted this lifestyle (Frändberg 1996, p. 32).

The material presented here shows that, despite differences between various groups, tourism travel is widely spread in the Swedish population and that it can therefore be seen as a primary consumer good (*op. cit.*, p. 35).

The Development of Outdoor Activities in Sweden 1976–91

What is noteworthy about the material in Figure 4.1 is that for the young in particular, but also for the middle-age groups (16–44), there is a break in the trend, with a decrease in outdoor activities and contact with nature over the period 1976–91. On the other hand, in the older age groups (45–74), with special emphasis on the oldest group, those over 65, there was a strong increase in outdoor activities over the period. It is interesting to see whether this tendency reflects a change of lifestyle in the different age groups. The diagram should at least reflect and give some indication of how various groups value different activities (cf. Sandell 1996a). A comparison between the trends in outdoor activities in Sweden in 1976–91 and those in holiday travel over the same period suggests that older age groups are more interested in and place greater value on outdoor activities. Trends in holiday travel show that the younger age groups make the most journeys and thus it may be assumed that they value this activity highly. The question is whether this can be explained by differences in lifestyles in a life-cycle perspective.

CONCLUSION: LIFESTYLE IN HOLIDAY TRAVEL AND SUSTAINABILITY

Levels of Mobility

Two groups of people emerge from the material we have considered, one that is not very mobile and one that is highly mobile. We may say that the groups have different lifestyles with regard to mobility during their leisure. These groups can also be related to two different aspects of sustainability. First, travel requires transport, which in itself has an impact on the environment. Second, there is also a connection with the hypothesis that the lifestyle and consumer patterns of tourists 'generate much more waste than the life the resident population leads' (Frändberg 1993, p. 21, my translation). This means that a group which is not particularly mobile, i.e. a group which travels relatively little, does not burden the environment as much as a highly mobile group does. It should be noted that this division into two groups is very general. The data show that it is advantaged people who are highly mobile. Typical of these individuals is that they have a good education, work in service professions and live in big cities.

Less mobile people

People with little mobility, i.e. with respect to holiday travel, are demographically primarily to be found in older age groups, those over 65. Further, they belong to so-called lower socio-economic groups, e.g. the early retired, the unemployed, single parents and farmers. From a geographical viewpoint, it is mainly those living in rural areas, e.g. in northern parts of Sweden, who are not very mobile. Apart from this, it may be noted that ill health can also lead to low mobility.

Highly mobile people

The corresponding features for highly mobile people are that demographically they belong to the younger age groups, 16–44, in particular young women. Socio-economically they are primarily senior salaried staff and they are away for longer periods and make more foreign trips than other groups. Geographically, they are big city dwellers, in particular from the Stockholm area. The difference between the two groups with respect to tourism travel tended to increase over the period 1976–91. Social developments since 1991 would suggest a continued increase in social differences, which would mean that the differences in holiday travel will also continue to increase. On the basis of the above presentation and discussion it may be concluded that phases in the life-cycle, material living standards, level of education and the geographical location of one's home produce different patterns of leisure travel.

PART 3

Tourism and Leisure Travel

CHAPTER 5

Mobility, Leisure Activities and Lifestyle

INTRODUCTION

Leisure and leisure activities play a major role in modern and late modern society. The general tendency is for such activities to be carried out at some distance from home. In Sweden almost 50% of the total volume of the transport of people is for leisure purposes (Vilhelmson 1990). In one sense a more sustainable society might be a society with less transportation and less mobility. One of a number of ways of achieving this is for leisure activities to be located close to home.

The primary aim of Part III, Tourism and Leisure Travel, is to describe the relation of lifestyle, leisure activities and mobility in the Swedish population today and the environmental impact of mobility. The study examines the mobility of different groups of people during their leisure and shows which leisure activities require mobility and which forms of transport are used. Since different forms of transport place different demands on resources such as fuel and use of land, consume more or less energy and have varying impacts on the environment in the form of emissions and noise, the study provides a basis for assessing the further consequences of our mobility in connection with leisure activities. Examples of energy consumption, environmental costs and environmental impact in relation to the choice of transport are given later.

AIM, ISSUES AND STRUCTURE OF THE SPECIAL STUDY[19]

The study concerns mobility and leisure activities, in particular the way in which travel is associated with what Swedes aged 20–64 do during their leisure time.

The aim is to provide an empirical illustration of mobility and leisure activities from a demographic perspective. The data are taken from SCB's time-use study from 1990–91.[20] One aspect which has been included in the presentation and analysis is how the leisure activities are related to the environment. The issues investigated in this study are: What proportion of the population have a lifestyle that presupposes mobility during leisure?[21] What are the typical features of the various mobility groups? Which leisure activities are especially dependent on mobility? We ask these questions in order to establish an empirical basis for discussing the effects limited mobility would have both on the individual's leisure and on the environment. The point of departure for the analysis is a simple segmentation of the population into groups who travel varying distances during their leisure time, i.e. who have different ranges of leisure activity space. Three mobility groups have been identified with respect to their actual leisure activity space. These groups are:

- Those active at home (at-home activity space). The people in this group perform their leisure activities at home, i.e. they are not mobile during their leisure time.
- Those active locally (local activity space). These people are active close to home.
- Those active at a distance (distant activity space). This group is active at some distance from home.

It should be noted that the individual's activity patterns depend on various kinds of resources and restrictions. The individual's activity patterns also vary over time and with type of community. The typical feature of leisure activities compared with many other types of activity, e.g. paid labour or household work, is that the individual can largely control and form them. To a not inconsiderable extent one can determine oneself how to spend one's leisure and where, and this means that one can, in this sense, steer one's lifestyle to more or less sustainable activities.

Figure 5.1 illustrates a leisure activity space. The range of a leisure activity space implicitly includes the individual's resources for and restrictions on travelling. The term leisure activity space is primarily applicable to relatively short-distance leisure travel. Long-distance tourism extends beyond the hinterland of the home district. This is illustrated in the figure by a trip from home to a main destination followed by a round trip. One strategy for achieving greater environmental sustainability is, as we mentioned above, to 'shrink' the activity space for tourism travel and leisure activities.

Using the home district as the point of departure, the figure illustrates a leisure activity space with various ranges, which are partly dependent on the time available and distance. The circles are not to scale. Leisure activity space is a valid concept

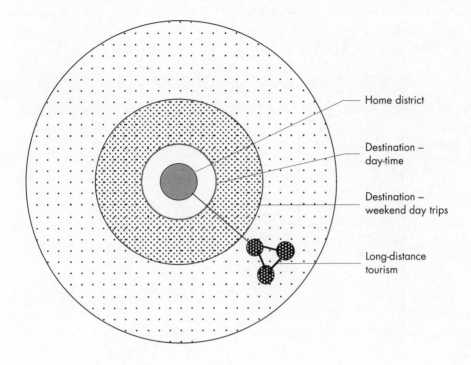

Home district

Destination –
day-time

Destination –
weekend day trips

Long-distance
tourism

Figure 5.1. A leisure activity space with various ranges.

primarily up to the level of weekend trips. The pattern of long-distance tourism is more a matter of links and nodes, as is indicated in the lower right-hand section of the figure.

THE DATA AND DEFINITIONS[22]

As already indicated, the empirical material used in this study is taken from SCB's time-use survey from 1990–91. The analysis concentrates on weekend leisure activities, which includes both Saturdays and Sundays. The respondents have been divided into three groups, defined in terms of the mobility their leisure activity space requires and evaluated from an overarching environmental perspective. The first group are those who, on the day they kept their diary, performed all their leisure activities at home. The second group are those who performed their leisure activities locally, travelling on foot, by bicycle or by local public transport. The third group are those who were largely dependent on their private cars for their leisure activities. An

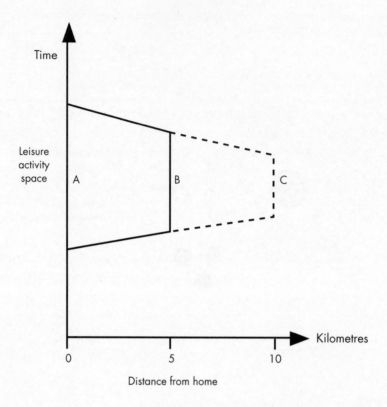

Figure 5.2. Time-geographical illustration of the groups: active at home (A), active locally (B) and active at a distance (C) and their different leisure activity spaces.

initial analysis of the data shows the distribution of the various forms of transport used for leisure activities according to distance from home. The use of the motor car for leisure activities increases dramatically somewhere in the interval 2.5–5 km from home. Travel on foot decreases considerably in the interval 5–10 km, with virtually nobody travelling on foot at 10 km. This observation provides a practical definition of the group that is active locally as people whose leisure activities can be reached and performed on foot, with the aid of a cycle or via local public transport. The highly mobile group of those active at a distance from home presupposes, in general, other means of transport such as the motor car or long-distance public transport. The arguments are illustrated in a time-geographical outline sketch (Figure 5.2) and operationalized to the following estimation of the sizes of the groups:

- People who limit their leisure activities to the home or its immediate vicinity account for 38% or 1380 individuals.
- People who are active locally, i.e. those who travel between 0.1 and 5 km from home in connection with their leisure activities, account for 11.1% or 404 individuals.
- People who are active at more distant locations and have travelled more than 5 km in connection with their leisure activities account for 50.9% or 1852 individuals.

It is important to realize that the figures in the survey are averages and this means that the same individuals do not always belong to one and the same group. The members of the groups vary from day to day; to what extent it is impossible to say on the basis of the existing data (which only describe the use of time in one 24-hour period and do not capture individual variations over the course of several days). Strictly speaking then, the groups can only be analysed at an aggregate group level and not at the level of the individual. The characteristic features of these groups will be analysed in respect of factors such as gender, age, type of household, home region, the significance of education and occupation, choice of transport, and leisure activities which require mobility, as well as the experience of stress.

RESULTS: MOBILITY AND LEISURE ACTIVITIES

The Significance of Gender

The active-at-home group consists of about equal proportions of men and women. There is, however, a certain tendency for men to perform their leisure activities farther from home than women, who are somewhat more active locally (see Table 5.1).

The Significance of Age

If the respondents are classified in the following age groups, 20–34, 35–49 and 50–64, the results show that the 35–49 group is most active at home, which is not surprising considering that this group contains a large proportion of families with children. However, there is a different pattern with regard to activity at a distance from home, where the youngest age group predominates, with the middle group in second place. On the other hand, activities at or near home, taken together, are more extensive in the middle and older age groups (see Table 5.1).

The Significance of Type of Household

A comparison between couples and single individuals shows that couples are more active at or near home than single people. Couples are also more active at or near home than at a distance from home. The opposite is true for single people (Table 5.1).

A comparison between households with and without children in the different age groups shows that households without children are considerably more active at a distance from home than those with children. Households where the youngest child is aged 0–6 have the lowest proportion of activities at a distance from home and the highest proportion at or near home compared with the other groups. Even in relative terms, this group has more activities at or close to home than at a distance from home. The same is true of the other households with children but to a lesser extent. Households without children are the only group who are more active at a distance from home than at or near home (see Table 5.1).

The Significance of the Home Region

Are there any regional differences? The point of departure in Table 5.1 is a division into so-called functional regions. Sweden has been divided into six regions with respect to population density (termed H-regions). The overall impression is that there are no major differences in distribution between the three activity groups during their leisure time. It may be noted that those living in the Stockholm region have the lowest proportion of leisure activities at home but most distant activities.

However, this regional division is very rough and does not really enable us to distinguish the various distance relations for individuals in the different types of region. However, the data may be used for another type of regional division and comparison. On the basis of a subjectively experienced dimension, the respondents in the survey indicate what type of area they live in, on a scale from purely rural area to dense urban area. This division reveals that those living in 'purely rural areas' and in 'villages or small places in the country' are more active at home and less active at a distance in comparison with other groups living in towns and cities. Distant activities are predominant in relation to activities at or near home in all the other groups. Those living in 'built-up areas with a mixture of single-family and multi-family housing' are the group that relatively speaking show the greatest difference between a small proportion of activities at or near home and the largest proportion of distant activities (see Table 5.1). We can establish, then, that those living in rural areas are more active at or near home than those living in towns.

A further aspect of the significance of where people live for their mobility pattern is whether or not they own, rent or have access to a weekend cottage. It is not particularly surprising that those who do not have access to a weekend cottage have a higher proportion of activities at or near home and fewer distant activities than those with access to a weekend cottage (see Table 5.1).

The Significance of Education and Occupation

An analysis of the importance of education for mobility during leisure time reveals the general pattern that the higher the level of education, the greater the percentage of activities at a distance from home, and the lower the level of education, the greater the proportion of activities at home or near home. The greatest proportion of distant activities and the lowest proportion of home activities are found in the group 'other tertiary education'. Thereafter come the groups 'three-year upper secondary school' and 'tertiary education, university/college' with the same pattern but not so pronounced as in the first group. The groups with 'two-year upper secondary school' and 'elementary/compulsory school' have the highest proportion of home activities and the lowest proportion of distant activities (see Table 5.1).

A breakdown of respondents' forms of employment shows that the group 'employed full-time' has a lower proportion of home activities and a higher proportion of distant activities than the group 'employed part-time'. It is also clear that the group 'farmer/assisting family member' has the highest proportion of home activities and the lowest proportion of distant activities of all the groups. The pattern is thus even more pronounced than for the group 'self-employed/assisting family member'. Those with the highest proportion of distant activities and the lowest proportion of home activities are 'students' (see Table 5.1).

The Use of Transport in the Leisure Activity Space

Households who own or have access to a motor car and those who do not are at a similar relative level as regards home activities. Those without a car have a considerably higher level of local activity than the other group and finally those with a car have a considerably higher level as regards distant activities (see Table 5.1).

As regards the groups who are mobile during their leisure time, i.e. those active locally and at a distance, the figures show that those active locally account for 10% of all journeys and those active at a distance for 90%. This means, then, that the latter group have made more journeys relative to their percentage of the population. The distribution of forms of transport and travel used during leisure time for both groups during the weekend is shown in Table 5.1. The table reveals the somewhat surprising result that the eco-friendly forms of travel, i.e. on foot, by cycle and by public transport, together account for 41% of people's leisure mobility at weekends. The absolutely predominant form of travel among those active locally is on foot and by cycle, 98%. In this respect then, this group may be said to be extremely eco-friendly. The motor car is the predominant form of transport among those active at a distance, 62% of the journeys, but the eco-friendly form of travel, on foot, by cycle and by public transport, together account for 35%, which is a surprisingly high figure.

Leisure Activities that Require Mobility

Table 5.1 also indicates the leisure activities that those active locally and at a distance, taken together, travel to. Journeys in connection with social intercourse can be seen to predominate, followed by journeys in connection with sports and outdoor activities, various kinds of walks, journeys in connection with club activities, culture and entertainment, and journeys to weekend cottages.

Table 5.1 also shows the travel pattern for leisure activities for those active locally and at a distance. Journeys in connection with social intercourse and various types of walks predominate in the group of those active locally, 83%. The main leisure activities for those active at a distance are journeys in connection with social intercourse and in connection with sports and outdoor activities. Due to the form of the survey, tourism only accounts for an insignificant percentage of leisure activities.

Of the journeys on foot made by those who are active locally, which total 92%, about half (45%) are 'walks in the woods and countryside' and 'other walks'. Apart from this, the material does not reveal how the choice of means of travel is related to leisure activities. An informed guess would suggest, however, that visits to friends and relatives, i.e. 'social intercourse' also tend to be made on foot.

The Experience of Stress in the Activity Groups

Questions regarding the experience of time pressure or stress were also included. These questions are, however, of a somewhat different nature from the previous material. The respondents were asked 'Do you usually have so much to do during the week that you have difficulty in doing everything that needs to be done?' Those who answered 'Yes, often' and 'No, never' respectively proved to be those who were most active at home and least active at a distance (see Table 5.1). The second question was: 'Are there things that you would like to do on weekdays but have to refrain from through lack of time?' It was the group that is most active at home and least active at a distance that answered 'Yes, often'. The group that is least active at home and most active at a distance answered 'No, seldom' (see Table 5.1). The answers are somewhat difficult to interpret but seem to suggest that it is primarily people in the active-at-home group that feel they do not have time and are thus forced to abstain from activities. The active-at-a-distance group is dominated by people who seldom have difficulty in doing everything they want to and are seldom forced to abstain from activities.

Table 5.1. Percentage distributions for different background variables by leisure activity space, i.e. for the population groups active at home, active locally and active at a distance, and totals. *Source*: Data from the Swedish Time-Use Survey 1990–91. Computerized by Aronsson & Vilhelmson (1998).

Background	Leisure activity space			Total	No. of people in survey population
	Active at home	Active locally	Active at a distance		
Gender					
• Men	37.3	8.2	54.5	100%	1833
• Women	38.5	14.3	47.2	100%	1803
Age					
• 20–34	34.6	8.7	56.7	100%	1297
• 35–49	40.5	11.1	48.4	100%	1401
• 50–64	38.5	14.7	46.8	100%	938
Type of household					
• Couples	40.1	11.0	48.9	100%	2683
• Single	32.4	11.6	56.0	100%	953
Households with or without children					
• No children	34.6	11.4	54.0	100%	1995
• Youngest child 0–6	45.2	10.1	44.7	100%	813
• Youngest child 7–12	40.8	9.8	49.4	100%	403
• Youngest child 13–18	37.6	13.4	49.0	100%	425
Functional home region					
• Stockholm (H1)	35.4	12.7	51.9	100%	521
• Göteborg and Malmö (H2)	40.3	10.7	49.0	100%	502
• Larger cities (H3)	37.6	10.7	51.7	100%	1276
• Southern intermediate areas (H4)	38.5	10.9	50.6	100%	825)
• Northern population centres (H5)	37.1	11.3	51.6	100%	248
• Northern rural areas (H6)	39.4	11.7	48.9	100%	264

Subjectively experienced home region	Leisure activity space			Total	No. of people in survey population
	Active at home	Active locally	Active at a distance		
• Purely rural area, only a few houses visible	43.9	9.9	46.2	100%	476
• Villages, small places in the country	44.5	9.3	46.2	100%	493
• Built-up areas, cities/suburbs with mainly detached or semi-detached housing	37.4	11.6	51.0	100%	1037
• Built-up areas, with detached and multi-family housing	35.7	8.8	55.5	100%	663
• Built-up areas, with mainly multi-family housing	34.0	14.2	51.8	100%	891
Weekend cottage[23]					
• Yes	35.2	10.7	54.1	100%	1440
• No	39.6	11.6	48.8	100%	2172
Level of education					
• Elementary/ compulsory school	38.9	13.0	48.1	100%	1286
• 2 yr upper secondary	40.0	9.5	50.5	100%	945
• 3 yr upper secondary	35.8	8.9	55.3	100%	561
• Tertiary education university/college	36.4	12.1	51.5	100%	735
• Other tertiary education	24.9	9.2	65.9	100%	88

Respondents' Occupation	Leisure activity space			Total	No. of people in survey population
	Active at home	Active locally	Active at a distance		
• Employed full-time	36.4	9.3	54.3	100%	2073
• Employed part-time	39.8	15.1	45.1	100%	685
• Self-employed/assisting family member	46.3	11.4	42.3	100%	253
• Farmer/assisting family member	54.2	9.4	36.4	100%	55
• On parental leave	42.1	14.2	43.7	100%	82
• On other leave	41.6	21.6	36.8	100%	28
• Student	19.6	13.7	66.7	100%	133
• On military service	38.7	0.0	61.3	100%	14
• Full-time work at home	45.4	15.1	39.5	100%	79
• Unemployed	41.0	8.8	50.2	100%	62
• Pension/disability pension, full/partial	38.9	14.6	46.5	100%	172

Car[24]					
• Yes	37.7	10.2	52.1	100%	3227
• No	39.0	18.7	42.3	100%	406

Means of/ transport travel[25]	Leisure activity space		Both groups	No. of trips
	Active locally	Active at a distance		
• Motor car	0	62.2	56.2	3513
• On foot	92.5	24.9	31.4	1905
• Public transport	0	6.5	5.9	336
• Cycle	5.1	3.2	3.3	207
• Unknown	1.3	2.2	2.1	133
• Air	0	0.6	0.6	33
• Ship	0	0.3	0.2	14
• Kick-sled	1	<0.1	0.1	11
• Motorcycle	0	<0.1	<0.1	2
• Moped	0	<0.1	<0.1	3
Total	100%	100%	100%	6157

Leisure activities[26]	Leisure activity space			No. of trips
	Active locally	Active at a distance	Both groups	
• Journeys in connection with sports and outdoor activities	4.2	14.2	13.2	820
• Journeys in connection with club activities	4.6	7.3	7.1	440
• Journeys in connection with culture and entertainment	6.5	6.6	6.6	401
• Journeys in connection with social intercourse	37.7	50.5	49.3	3019
• Journeys in connection with television and radio	0	0.1	0.1	7
• Journeys in connection with hobbies	0	<0.1	2.0	123
• Journeys in connection with reading	0.8	2.1	0	2
• Walks in the woods and countryside	8.0	3.0	3.5	219
• Other walks	37.4	6.9	9.9	615
• Cycling	0.6	0.6	0.6	39
• Boat trips	0	0.2	0.2	10
• Car trips	0	0.6	0.5	30
• Journeys to weekend cottage, weekend journeys	0.2	7.7	6.9	416
• Tourism	0	0.3	0.2	16
Total	100%	100%	100%	6157

Difficulty in getting everything done	Leisure activity space			Total	No. of people in survey population
	Active at home	Active locally	Active at a distance		
• Yes, often	39.9	9.6	50.5	100%	1345
• Yes, sometimes	37.1	11.0	51.9	100%	1038
• No, seldom	33.7	13.8	52.5	100%	633
• No, never	39.3	12.0	48.7	100%	604

Forced to refrain from activities

• Yes, often	41.2	8.6	50.2	100%	1013
• Yes, sometimes	37.5	11.5	51.0	100%	1247
• No, seldom	34.4	12.7	52.8	100%	471
• No, never	36.9	12.7	50.4	100%	878

CONCLUDING REMARKS ON MOBILITY AND LEISURE ACTIVITIES

The Person Who is Active at Home/Locally and the Person Who is Active at a Distance

On the basis of the above results, it is possible to give a rough general picture of the typical characteristics of the person who is active at or near home and the person who is active at a distance in contemporary Swedish society. To put it in other terms, during their leisure time the different groups of people have a lifestyle that may be characterized as active at home/locally or active at a distance (see Table 5.2).

Table 5.2. The predominant characteristics of the person who is active at home/locally and at a distance respectively. These characteristics are based on the time-use data for leisure activities at weekends (Saturdays and Sundays).

The person who is active at home/locally	The person who is active at a distance
• Female	• Male
• Age: 35–49	• Age: 20–34
• Living with a partner	• Living alone
• With small children	• With no children
• Living in the country	• Living in the city
• With little education	• Highly educated
• Part-time work in agriculture or otherwise self-employed	• White-collar worker/student
• Does not have access to a car	• Has access to a car
• Does not have access to a weekend cottage	• Has access to a weekend cottage

The statements in Table 5.2 should only be interpreted as typical features of the groups at an aggregate level. The nature of the data makes it impossible to comment on particular individuals or for them to belong to one and the same group throughout.

Environmental Aspects of Mobility and Leisure Activities

The division of the population into the three groups, those active at home, locally and at a distance, emphasizes the mobility aspects of leisure activities; it is also useful for discussing environmental aspects of the lifestyles of Swedish people through a consideration of their choice of means of transport for leisure travel and the consequent impact on the environment. If we only take into account mobility in connection with leisure activities and ignore the consumption of resources and the impact on the environment involved in the leisure activity, it may be claimed that those who are active at or near home are the most eco-friendly in their leisure activities. Yet this does not take into consideration the underlying structural conditions which force certain groups to pursue leisure activities at or near home. If they had the opportunity, these groups might well show the same pattern of activity as those who are active at a distance from home. For the material shows that it is those who are active at or close to home that experience most stress, which might suggest that they are dissatisfied with their situation and would prefer different temporal–spatial structural conditions. The material shows that it is those with resources who are the most mobile.

A general conclusion that can be drawn from the data and the analysis is that, to achieve environmentally sustainable development for the high level of mobility during leisure time, we must either use other forms of transport than those that predominate at present or travel shorter distances and perform more leisure activities locally. An alternative would be to reduce the frequency of journeys, i.e. stay away longer once we have reached our weekend cottage, for instance. Another point concerns changes in the institutional and structural systems. Examples include the technical development of the various means of transport, alterations to and the reorganization of the transport system and the development of tourism and leisure activities in the vicinity of population centres.

CHAPTER 6

The High Level of Mobility in the Rich World

DISTRIBUTIONAL PERSPECTIVES ON MOBILITY AND THE ENVIRONMENT

A high level of mobility of goods and people in the world is closely linked with the emergence of modern society and economic growth. One question that immediately springs to mind is whether this high level of mobility of goods and people across the globe is a sign of development and, above all, sustainable development. Whitelegg puts it in the following terms:

> The impact of transport on society is better understood through a general appreciation of the links among consumption, economic growth, environmental impact and sustainability. The demand for transport is closely linked to measures of economic growth and the sustainability debate raises fundamental questions about the viability of a long-term increase in the demand for transport and the possibility that transport might in some way be curtailed (i.e. demand reduced) while the economy continues to grow. (Whitelegg 1993, p. 2)

The environmental crisis facing the world may be said to be a crisis of sustainability which has been primarily caused by the systems of production and consumption in the rich world and their accompanying lifestyles; and these, in their turn, are imitated, to the greatest possible extent, by the majority of poor countries. The high level of mobility in the rich world contrasts strongly with the lack of mobility in the poor world.

Sustainability means adjustment in lifestyles and structures to bring about a reduction in the consumption of the North and an increase in the consumption of the South. Transport is at the core of this process because it defines the spatial and temporal boundaries of production and consumption . . . (Whitelegg 1993, p. 13)

There is an aspect of social distribution in our efforts to conquer distances in a shorter time. It is the rich elite of the world who have this privilege. In this respect, the poor are living at the same level as they did a hundred years ago; they possibly have the time, but they do not have the money to travel to any great extent. Currently only 8 per cent of the world's population (mainly the rich world) own a car. From the standpoint of sustainability, with increased resource consumption, air pollution, noise and demand for land it is scarcely conceivable that car ownership could be fairly distributed among the people of the world. It should also be noted that, in terms of sustainability and equality, the increased ownership and use of the motor car in the rich world is not a relevant issue, for the same reasons as above. However, politically reducing the use of cars is difficult for a number of reasons, in particular because: 'The motor car is important as a bearer of symbols, both outwardly (status symbol) and inwardly (as an expression of a person's self-perception)' (Wärneryd *et al.* 1995, p. 60, my translation). Wärneryd *et al.* go on to say: 'There is much to suggest that mobility is the factor which will be most difficult to cope with in the efforts to change society in a more sustainable direction' (*ibid.*, p. 116, my translation).

A further issue is whether technical developments can reduce the impact on the environment. Whitelegg argues that technical progress in the area of transport will not be sufficient to achieve the desired reduction in environmental impact, but that what is needed instead are changes in lifestyles and in the transport system and other social structures (Whitelegg 1993, p. 8). However, on the one hand, technical developments necessitate a revision of estimates of the consumption of resources. On the other, development leads to new environmental problems; for instance, new chemical compounds in products, when used on a large scale, lead to new waste disposal problems. Technical progress is important but it raises a number of questions. Will it on its own solve the resource and environmental problems or are changes in lifestyles also necessary? How can we solve the problems of distribution between rich and poor countries? Will technical progress lead to a bigger gap because the majority of the world's population will not be able to afford the innovations?

If man is not to consume the earth's resources, no more than about half a billion people can have a material standard equivalent to ours, according to an assessment based on the calculations of the Dag Hammarskjöld Fund in 1976. (Miljödepartementet 1991, p. 6, my translation)

The world already has many more inhabitants, 5.7 billion (Worldwatch Institute 1996, p. 7), and there is great inequality between rich and poor. It is obvious that from an environmental perspective it is impossible for all the people in the world to achieve the living standards of the rich world, measured in the terms that we traditionally use today and with the type of resource utilization and waste disposal that is predominant. A more relevant strategy than concentrating on efforts to increase material living standards would be for the people of the rich world to change their lifestyle to one that is environmentally sustainable and for the earth's resources and other assets to be more equitably distributed than is the case today.

THE CONSEQUENCES OF THE HIGH LEVEL OF MOBILITY

Introduction

> Time . . . is central to notions of sustainability. A sustainable city or a sustainable transport policy or a sustainable economy cannot be founded on economic principles which through their monetarization of time orientate society towards higher levels of motorization, faster speed and greater consumption of space. The fact that these characteristics produce energy intensive societies and pollution is only part of the problem. More importantly these characteristics distort value systems, elevate mobility above accessibility, associate higher speeds with progress and lower speeds with anti-modernism and dislocate communities and social life. (Whitelegg 1993, p. 96)

How we organize our everyday life and leisure, including the use of resources and disposal of waste, has consequences for the spatial organization of society and mobility. In its turn, high mobility with the primary means of transport used in the rich world today results in a set of environmental consequences which cannot be characterized as sustainable. I maintain therefore that, in order to solve the environmental problems of mobility, we must go to the root of the problems, i.e. to the organization of social life. Whitelegg makes a comparison between society in the 1990s and in the 1920s and comments:

> What is clear is that we must travel further to make contact with work, shops, schools and places of recreation. Since we are able to increase distances between things like hospitals, schools, and shopping centres (and this is the direct result of much public and private decision making), but not increase the numbers of hours in the day, then we increase speed. Basically we use technology to permit greater speeds but still work, eat, sleep and play in roughly the same proportions as always. We simply do these things further apart from each other. (Whitelegg 1993, p. 76)

An ever-increasing geographical mobility, in the transport of both goods and people, has been one of the distinctive features of industrial society over the last hundred years. The following is an example: in 1950 a Swede travelled on average 9 km per day. The equivalent distances in 1985 were 33 km and in 1990, 40 km per day (Wärneryd *et al.* 1995, p. 53). Mobility is connected with two reciprocal processes: on the one hand, structural change in society and, on the other, the actor's, the individual's, choice of activity pattern, which is an expression of lifestyle. The development of mobility can be illustrated in the form of three time sections (see Figure 6.1). The first is an example of the mobility pattern in the agricultural society of 1850. The second is from early industrial society in 1900 and the third from late industrial society in 1975. In the first case most of the everyday activities were carried out in the immediate proximity of the home with few and slow journeys. Society was characterized by geographical stability (Vilhelmson 1990). In the second example, early industrial society, it was primarily people's mobility that increased, particularly journeys to work. Society was characterized by limited mobility. Continued social development led to a clear division of functions and urbanization. This together with the development of the means of transport and cheap energy cooperated to produce geographical flexibility (Vilhelmson 1990; Wärneryd *et al.* 1995, pp. 55–7).

> A very rough classification suggests that the environmental problems of the western world are increasingly due to traffic, the consumption of goods, the use of chemicals and waste disposal. In eastern Europe spot emissions from the chimneys and sewers of industrial plants and power stations are still the predominant problem, whilst the problems of the developing countries are mainly linked with the exploitation of natural resources. (Miljödepartementet 1991, p. 8, my translation)

In many of the industrial nations of the Western world, 'large-scale' purification techniques are well developed, e.g. sewage treatment and the cleansing of industrial emissions. Generally speaking, there are more problems with the many small and dispersed emissions in connection, for instance, with transport and the waste disposal of consumer goods (see Figure 6.2).

There are two global 'systems' which provide the conditions for life on earth and which we disrupt in various ways through our activities. The first is the atmosphere, which functions more or less like a greenhouse. Without it the mean temperature on earth would be much lower. The existence of the so-called greenhouse effect is at present the subject of much discussion among scientists. According to Naturvårdsverket, new information has emerged in recent years which has resulted in general agreement among the scientific community that

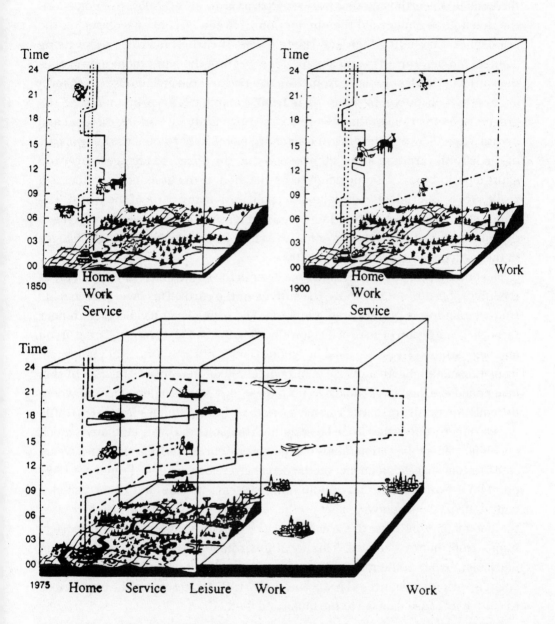

Figure 6.1. Three time sections (1850, 1900 and 1975) which show daily mobility.
Source: Wärneryd *et al.* (1995, pp. 55–7)

the climate on earth is getting warmer (Naturvårdsverket 1995a, p. 6). In short, the debate has concerned the connection between 'greenhouse gases' in the atmosphere, including high and rising levels of carbon dioxide, and a rising average temperature. This means that energy from the sun's radiation reaches the earth but that less radiates from the earth because the greenhouse gases form a cover which prevents some of it from escaping. The proponents of the greenhouse effect claim that it is reinforced primarily by burning oil, coal and natural gas and by transport. The counter argument is that global warming is part of the natural variation in the climate and that the observed changes cover too short a period for a valid decision to be reached. If the greenhouse effect is a reality, there is a risk of major climatic changes in many parts of the world. The consequences may vary from increased drought in certain areas to increased precipitation in others. Further, some areas may become colder through changes in the main ocean currents (Flavin 1996).

The other global 'system' is the ozone layer in the stratosphere, which is part of the atmosphere 10–50 km above the surface of the earth. This layer protects life from certain forms of ultraviolet radiation. The ozone layer has become thinner through the emission of so-called chlorofluorocarbon (CFC) compounds, e.g. freon and halocarbons. These are used in, among things, refrigerators, heat pumps and insulating materials. An increase in ultraviolet radiation increases the risk of skin cancer and eye damage. Damage to both these 'systems' is independent of where the emission occurs on earth, i.e. they are global. Exhaust fumes from road traffic do not directly affect the ozone layer in the stratosphere. However, there is much uncertainty about the various kinds of atmospheric emissions from air traffic, where some results suggest an impact on the ozone layer (Archer 1993; Frändberg 1996, pp. 44–7). Furthermore, air-conditioning systems in cars and other vehicles contribute to the negative impact on the ozone layer. Road traffic also increases the amount of ozone close to the earth. In cities the emissions are primarily exhaust fumes from motor vehicles. This local environmental problem is caused, in particular, by air pollutants, such as nitrogen oxides and hydrocarbons, and by volatile organic substances like solvents and petrol. An increase in the ozone close to earth may cause damage to the fauna and flora.

Transportrådet (the Transport Council) has provided information on developments in the transport of people, i.e. the total distance travelled in Sweden from 1950 onwards, with a forecast up to the year 2020 (Miljödepartementet 1991, pp. 230–1). The figures show an enormous increase over the period. In 1950 Swedish people travelled a total of about 25 billion passenger-kilometres, of which the motor car accounted for about 5 billion. The equivalent figure in the forecast for 2020 is almost 160 billion person-kilometres, of which the motor car accounts for almost

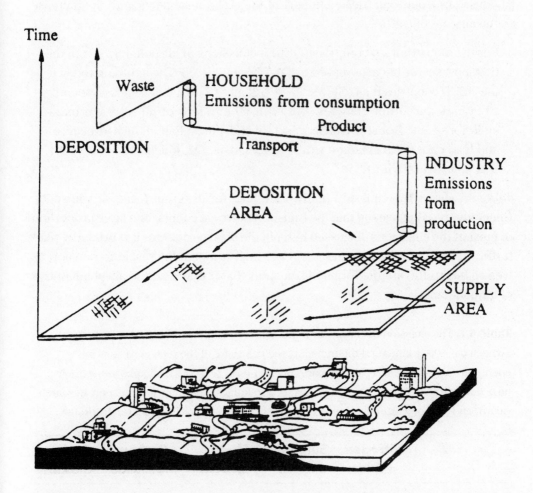

Figure 6.2. The flow of resources, supply area and deposition area.
Source: Wärneryd *et al.* (1995, p. 14)

120 billion. Public transport shows only a moderate increase. It is long-distance journeys, over 100 km, that account for and, according to the forecast, will account for the biggest increase, and long-distance car journeys will show the greatest absolute increase. It is estimated, however, that air transport will account the greatest relative increase.

Air Pollution

Air pollution is one of the most serious environmental consequences of transport and road transport in particular. Exhaust emission control has led to a reduction in emissions from road traffic but part of the effect disappears with the increase in the amount of traffic.

For the industrialized countries (OECD) emissions of air pollutants from the transport sector have increased by 20–75% since 1975. The situation today in the OECD countries is as follows: 70–90% of all carbon dioxide emissions come from cars and other vehicles. Between 60 and 80% of all nitrogen oxide emissions come from the transport sector and almost half of the hydrocarbon and lead emissions emanate from car exhausts. (Miljödepartementet 1991, p. 234, my translation)

Table 6.1 shows the emission of air pollutants for different forms of transport. Generally speaking, we see that the transport sector accounts for a large proportion of most of the emissions discussed here. In the transport sector it is primarily road traffic, in particular private cars, that have high emission figures. Rail transport as well as bus traffic are the forms of transport that produce the smallest quantities of air pollutants.

Table 6.1. The emission of certain air pollutants from different forms of transport in Sweden per 1000 tonnes and the transport sector's share of the total emissions in the country in 1987–88. *Source*: Miljödepartementet (1991, p. 235). The figures are, in their turn, taken from Naturvårdsverket, Transportforskningsberedningen (Transport Research Board) and Väg- och Trafikforsknings Institutet (Road and Traffic Research Institute).

	Nitrogen oxides	Sulphur dioxide	Hydro-carbons	Carbon monoxide	Carbon dioxide
Road traffic (tonnes)	183	11	174	994	17 700
Of this: private cars	111	–	156	908	12 200
lorries	58	–	16	84	4 600
buses	13	–	1	2	800
Civil shipping	33	17	2	2	600
Of this: ferries	20	11	–	–	–
Civil air traffic	7	–	3	8	2 100
Rail transport	1	<1	<1	<1	170
Other mobile sources	71	5	16	42	3 731
Other sources	84	180	203	320	40 300
The transport sector's share of total emissions	60%	13%	51%	78%	32%

Road traffic is the dominant source of emissions of nitrogen oxides. These emissions have shown a considerable increase mainly because of the increase in motoring since the 1950s, but have stagnated in recent years. Catalytic exhaust emission control has reduced the emissions from each individual car but, at the same time, the number of cars and journeys has increased significantly. Nitrogen oxide emissions from cars have only been reduced by 9 per cent since 1980, despite the fact that about half of all private cars have catalytic emission control (Naturvårdsverket 1995a, p. 31). Catalysts cannot as yet be used on diesel engines to reduce nitrogen oxide emissions. These emissions result in acidification, eutrophication and an increase in ground-level ozone.

Sulphur dioxide emissions have significantly decreased in Sweden since the 1970s. Even the transport sector's share of these emissions has been somewhat reduced. The major factors in this decrease are the stricter regulations regarding the level of sulphur in oil and the reduced use of oil. In road traffic, sulphur dioxide emissions are mainly produced by diesel-driven vehicles and this may account for a large proportion of the emissions in built-up areas. The effect of this type of emission on people is an increased risk of bronchial diseases. Nitrogen oxides and sulphur are the main causes of acidification in nature.

Hydrocarbons and nitrogen oxides together with the conversion products they give rise to are especially dangerous to people, with an increased risk of infections etc. (Miljödepartementet 1991, p. 236). In the larger cities car exhaust fumes account for about 60 per cent of these emissions. Hydrocarbons can be largely removed by means of the catalyst technique.

In built-up areas cars account for the major share of carbon monoxide emissions. Carbon monoxide prevents the blood from assimilating and transporting oxygen, which increases the risk of cardiovascular diseases, among other things.

The level of carbon dioxide in the atmosphere has increased by 29 per cent since the mid-1800s (Naturvårdsverket 1995a, p. 6). Carbon dioxide emissions from the transport sector have shown a significant increase since the 1970s. Altogether, i.e. all sectors of society included, these emissions have, however, decreased radically in Sweden since the 1970s. Carbon dioxide contributes, among other things, to the greenhouse effect and it cannot be removed by catalysts.

Other air pollutants which should be mentioned in this context are volatile organic compounds, an umbrella term for many different substances. They are carcinogenic, can damage the genetic make-up and nervous system, and produce allergies. Traffic is the major source of these emissions (Miljödepartementet 1991, pp. 44–5).

Noise

The higher noise levels in recent years are in the main the result of the increase in road traffic. This is especially noticeable in built-up areas. Noise is usually measured in decibels on a logarithmic scale. 65dB(A) has been set as the average daily upper limit for noise. To give some examples, the average level of noise close to a motorway is about 70dB(A). Lorries, motorcycles and underground trains produce a noise level of about 90dB(A) and an aircraft taking off about 120dB(A). According to an estimate from the Organization for Economic Cooperation and Development, about 130 million people in the OECD countries are exposed to an unacceptable level of noise, i.e. over 65dB(A), and about 400 million in the same area are exposed to noise above 55dB(A) (Whitelegg 1993, p. 61). The proportion of the population exposed to a level above 65dB(A) varies between countries and areas, for instance 5% of the population in parts of Scandinavia are said to be exposed to unacceptable levels compared with 30% in the urban areas of Europe. On the other hand, the proportion of the population who think the outdoor noise level during the day-time is acceptable, i.e. less than 55dB(A), is less than 20% in urban areas of Europe but over 60% in Scandinavia (Whitelegg 1993, p. 64). According to Naturvårdsverket's estimates, between one and three million people are disturbed on a daily basis by noise from road traffic in Sweden (Miljödepartementet 1991, p. 236). However, rail and air traffic make more noise than road traffic if each individual unit is measured. There are major local noise problems close to airports but there is a good chance that this noise can be reduced through the introduction of new types of aircraft.

Different vehicles produce different levels of noise. The primary sources of noise in road traffic are the engine, ventilation system, transmission, tyre friction, brakes and load. Technical solutions are being developed for all these sources of noise (Whitelegg 1993, pp. 66–7). Of road vehicles it is lorries and motorcycles that produce the most noise. According to Whitelegg, measures to reduce the noise produced by these two types of vehicles have a greater effect than general measures for reducing noise in vehicles. The factors which together determine the noise level of a vehicle are its speed and type. The import of the above is that if more goods and people were transported by rail instead of by road, there would be a reduction in noise (Whitelegg 1993, p. 64).

Noise restricts the opportunities for social life in public areas, making it more difficult to carry on a conversation and, in general, more unpleasant to be outdoors. Social life is also affected in that road traffic leads to a deterioration in the conditions for pedestrians and cyclists (Whitelegg 1993, p. 69). Noise affects people in different ways; their hearing may be damaged for instance, or it may cause stress reactions and affect sleep.

Apart from altering vehicles, measures to reduce noise include constructing bypasses around built-up areas, putting a 'price' on noise, setting up noise barriers or planting trees and bushes, separating footpaths and cycle paths from other road traffic, speed limits, political decisions which favour public transport, pedestrians and cyclists, and noise-reducing road surfacing material.

The Use of Land

> Our propensity to travel longer distances by car and our reliance on lorries to carry large amounts of freight on which our lifestyle depends have created a land-use structure and a set of expectations that make transport policies one of the most intractable of policy areas. (Whitelegg 1993, p. 1)

As the above quotation suggests, the spatial organization of modern society with its division of functions and a globally specialized division of labour is a precondition for the high level of mobility. The current direction in which society is moving does not suggest any major changes in this respect. This, in its turn, places almost deterministic demands on land-use for the infrastructure of mobility. It is clear that our 'high-speed society' entails an extensive consumption of space for the infrastructure that is a precondition for movement.

Whitelegg (1993, p. 78) suggests that the greater the speed of the means of transport, the greater the consumption of space is likely to be. Further, he argues that there is a connection between high speed and high social status. One example is that the over-full diary, which demands rapid transportation between activities, is a sign of high social standing.

The infrastructure of the transport system affects the landscape in both the urban and rural environments and may result in a negative impact on sensitive natural environments. Generally speaking road traffic demands more land than rail traffic. Roads and railways also produce barrier effects, i.e. they may be difficult for both people and animals to cross. Airports and ports are also dominant features in the landscape and require extensive traffic networks for connecting ground transport.

According to Kane, the most decisive factor in limiting the future use, primarily, of the motor car, but also of road traffic in general, is the extensive use of land for roads and parking areas (Kane 1996, p. 186). This factor is particularly crucial in densely populated Asia, where land-use for the transport system is in direct conflict with the cultivable land required for survival.

Summary of the Consequences of the High Level of Mobility

To summarize, the emission of air pollutants is one of the most serious environmental problems caused by mobility and the transport system. Other negative impacts are noise and the great demand for land. The various

Table 6.2. Summary of some of the most significant environmental impacts of the transport sector. *Source*: Miljödepartementet (1991, p. 234).

	Local impacts or impacts in built-up areas	**Regional impacts**	**Global impacts**
Air pollutants	*Ill health* Cancer Bronchial diseases Cardiovascular diseases Nervous diseases Reduced immune defence Allergies	*Ill health* Higher levels of metals in ground water	*Ill health* Increased risk of skin cancer
	Damage to plants Trees Plantations	*Damage to plants* Trees Herbs Crops	*Damage to plants* Damage to leaves and needles Changes in distribution
	Corrosion Buildings Paper etc	*Corrosion* Water/sewage system Electricity and telephone cables	*Effects on the climate* Changes in temperature
Water pollutants	*Damage to plants*	*Eutrophication of ocean environments* *Effects on marine environments* (e.g. oil tanker accidents)	
Use of land	*Barrier effects*	*Impact on the landscape*	*Risk of genetic/species impoverishment*
Noise	*Impact on the urban scene* *Disturbance of sleep* Reduced capacity for work	*Impact on sensitive natural environments*	

environmental impacts produced by the transport sector have different ranges. Table 6.2 gives examples of some of the most serious environmental impacts of the transport sector as regards range. The various air pollutants and noise from road traffic produce local environmental impacts. Regional environmental impacts include eutrophication and acidification, which are caused by sulphur dioxide and nitrogen dioxides among others. These regional environmental effects can be partially limited by local measures since the problems are largely 'imported'. Finally, the greenhouse effect is an example of a global environmental impact to which transport contributes through the emission of carbon dioxide.

A further aspect is the costs which are incurred as a result of injuries and deaths caused by traffic. It may be noted that the proportion of serious injuries increases with the speed of the vehicle involved in the accident (Whitelegg 1993, p. 86). This point will not be considered further here.

AN ENVIRONMENTALLY ADAPTED TRANSPORT SYSTEM

In 1994 a number of interest groups began working together in Sweden to devise a strategy for long-term sustainability, i.e. a transport system that was adapted to the environment.[27] There were three core issues: first, what was meant by an environmentally adapted transport system and what environmental goals were to be met; second, what needed to be changed in order to meet the environmental goals for the transport sector; and third, how the changes were to be implemented and what control mechanisms should be used (Naturvårdsverket 1996a, p. 7). The objective was for the changes to be implemented over a 25–30-year period.

The proposed measures for achieving the environmental goals of the transport sector are grouped into five areas, where the first relates to 'measures to reduce the need for transport'. Here, among other things, it is suggested that the use of information technology and other measures will result in more work being carried out at home and thus fewer journeys to work, that the division of functions in the community between home – work – service – leisure activities must be reduced and that there must be an increase in the national, regional and local production of goods and services, thereby reducing the need for transport.

The second area covers 'measures to improve distribution and cooperation between forms of transport'. Under this heading, it is suggested that, as far as the transportation of people is concerned, there should be a greater concentration of buildings, more coordination between the different forms of transport with, for instance, traffic nodes for transfer from one form to another and a shift from forms of transport with a high negative impact on the environment to those that have a less negative impact.

Table 6.3. Threats against the environment from the transport sector and the preliminary goals for the sector for the year 2020. *Source*: Naturvårdsverket (1996a, pp. 17–19).

Threats	Preliminary environmental goals for the transport sector for 2020
Climatic effects	Ten per cent reduction of the emission of carbon dioxide from fossil fuels compared with 1990.
Depletion of the ozone	There will be no emission of gases that can damage the ozone layer in the stratosphere.
Acidification of land and water	Ninety per cent reduction of sulphur emissions compared with 1980. Eighty per cent reduction of nitrogen oxide emissions compared with 1980.
Photochemical oxidants/ground-level ozone	Eighty-five per cent reduction of emissions of volatile organic compounds compared with 1988. Eighty per cent reduction of nitrogen oxide emissions compared with 1980.
Air pollution and noise in urban areas (local problems)	For noise – Naturvårdsverket's long-term goals. Emissions of carcinogenic substances to be reduced by 50 per cent as a first step. The maximum permissible values for nitrogen oxide and carbon monoxide to be achieved. The maximum permissible values to be determined so that valuable buildings and monuments can be protected.
Eutrophication of land and water	Emissions of urea from airports will have ceased. Eighty per cent reduction in nitrogen oxide emissions compared with 1980.
Impact of metals	The national goals also cover the transport sector. Measures are being devised within the framework for adaptation of the transport system to recycling.
Introduction and spread of foreign organisms	The unintentional introduction of foreign species will not occur.
Use of land and water as a production resource	The goals have not as yet been determined.
Exploitation of land and water for building, plant and infrastructure	The transport sector will have been adapted to the long-term conservation of natural resources with respect to the use of materials and the exploitation of land which is important for recreation, particularly land which is close to urban areas. The historical structures and physical geographical relations of cities, urban areas and the landscape will have been preserved and will be apprehensible in the forms that are characteristic of the various regions of the country.
Claims on particularly valuable areas (certain cultivated areas worth protecting)	The transport system will have been adapted in accordance with the restrictions established for the protection of natural and cultural landscapes and environments.
Broken cycles, waste and dangerous waste (adapting the transport system to cycles)	The transport system in the broadest sense will have been adapted to the natural cycles of energy and material. The products cycle within the technosphere will have been detoxicated.

The third area is termed 'measures to improve the function of each of the forms of transport', i.e. road and rail traffic, air traffic and shipping. The fourth area provides for 'technical improvements to vehicles regarding such matters as fuel'. Finally, the fifth area is 'measures to improve the expansion, running and maintenance of infrastructures'. In the last two cases each form of traffic is considered separately (Naturvårdsverket 1996a, appendix 1).

The individual measures in the five areas indicated above have, in their turn, been brought together in three 'packages', which have as their point of departure the attainment of as many of the environmental goals as possible. The 'basic package' includes changes resulting from decisions that have already been taken or decisions that it is assumed will be taken within the next few years. This basic package is, however, insufficient for the attainment of the environmental goals so two further packages with a very different emphasis have been suggested. The 'traffic package' includes measures that affect the extent, localization and management of traffic and the impact of building, running and maintaining infrastructures. The 'technical package', in its turn, includes measures that are concerned with the technical improvement of vehicles and fuels. None of these packages will, it is assumed, resolve all the threats against the environment; it is rather that a combination of measures is needed.

Table 6.3 details the threats to the environment from the transport sector and the preliminary goals for the year 2020.

CHAPTER 7

Forms of Transport and the Environmental Consequences of Tourism and Leisure Travel

INTRODUCTION

Tourism and leisure travel must be considered in a social context where lifestyles and consumer patterns provide a background for an understanding of these phenomena. This background and context have been demonstrated in previous chapters. Tourism and leisure travel presuppose that we travel a certain distance from home during a certain period of time. For this purpose we use all conceivable forms of transport. We have previously given an account of the forms of transport used by Swedes for both domestic and foreign leisure travel and this subject will also be further discussed later. To summarize, the distribution shows a clear predominance for the motor car for domestic travel and some predominance for air transport over the car for foreign travel (cf. Page 1994). The consequences of the choice of transport for tourist travel, which correspond well with the general picture of the impact of the transport system presented above, are described by Kosters in the following manner:

1) Heavy traffic congestion. This occurs already on motorways to major tourist destinations, mainly on the primary north-south motorways. Particularly in France and Western Germany, it is not unusual to have one horrendous traffic jam extending 100 kilometres or more during peak tourist periods. During holiday seasons there is also considerable congestion at European airports and in their air corridors. Congestion is also increasing inside popular tourist destinations, such as along the Mediterranean coasts during summer and in the Alpine region in the snow season.

2) Pollution effects. New roads and motorways cut the landscape and nature to pieces and parking lots often create visual pollution. Vehicle engines severely pollute the environment and tourist towns with exhaust fumes. Noise, also a serious type of pollution, is produced within motorways and air corridors as well as in more pastoral settings.

3) Erosion of natural amenities. The growth of tourism requires scenery, landscape, and nature for the increasing number of tourists. New tourist areas are continuously being developed to add to the existing ones. But sometimes planning systems are very poorly conceived, as can be observed in Greece and Turkey, and sometimes they are overwhelmed by visitor volumes, including those visitors' transportation needs. Dependence on traditional means of transport such as the automobile, creates a conflict between the amenities by those wishing to enjoy them.

Tourism growth, therefore, often damages parts of its major attraction as a side effect of the modes of transport it encourages. Particularly in densely populated Europe, this poses a serious challenge that is not easily resolved. In Europe, where about 80 percent of holiday travel is presently done by automobile and about 10 percent by airplane, transport mode related problems continue to mount. The train, in contrast, which is the least environmentally damaging of all major forms of tourist transport, captures only a small percent of the tourism market. (Kosters 1992, p. 183)

According to Frändberg's survey (1996), the use of the car, measured in travel frequency, is the predominant means of transport for long-distance travel (see Table 7.1). Furthermore, in terms of travel frequency, the car is used for 68% of tourist journeys. On the other hand, in terms of the distance travelled on long journeys, the importance of the car is not so marked. Air transport, which only accounts for 8% of long journeys when travel frequency is measured, becomes more dominant at 43% when the unit of measurement is person-kilometres (see Table 7.2). This measure demonstrates the importance of the relatively few but long international journeys where air transport accounts for 62% of the leisure journeys measured in person-kilometres (Frändberg 1996, pp. 27, 29). Given that air transport is so predominant when it comes to long-distance journeys measured in person-kilometres, Frändberg points out that emissions from aircraft and their environmental effects are underestimated in the current debate on the environment (*ibid.*, pp. 44–6). The overall figures show that car and air transport in connection with tourism journeys are of considerable significance in a discussion of mobility and environmental consequences.

Table 7.1. Number (in millions) of journeys and proportion of long-distance travel (over 100 km one-way) according to purpose and means of transport according to the survey of travel habits, 1994. *Source*: Frändberg (1996, p. 27).

| | **Means of Transport** | | | | | | | | |
Purpose of journey	Car	Air	Train	Bus	Ship	Other	No Info.	Total	%
Leisure, of this:									
Visits to relatives/ friends	11.0	0.8	1.9	0.5	0.2	0.1	0	14.5	23
Weekend cottage	6.6	0.1	0.2	0.2	0.1	0	0	7.2	12
Tourism	12.9	1.7	1.1	2.1	0.9	0.2	0	18.9	30
Service	1.8	0	0.1	0.1	0	0	0	2.1	3
Work	9.6	2.5	1.8	0.9	0.2	0.3	0	15.3	25
Other/ no information	1.5	0.1	0.5	0.3	0	0.1	1.7	4.3	7
Total	43.5	5.3	5.6	4.2	1.4	0.7	1.7	62.4	100
%	70	8	9	7	2	1	3	100	

Table 7.2. Distribution in billions of person-kilometres and proportion of long-distance travel (over 100 km one-way) according to purpose and means of transport according to the survey of travel habits, 1994. *Source*: Frändberg (1996, p. 27).

| | **Means of Transport** | | | | | | | |
Purpose of journey	Car	Air	Train	Bus	Ship	Other	Total	%
Leisure, of this:								
Visits to relatives/ friends	5.2	2.2	1.2	0.3	0.2	0	9.1	19
Weekend cottage	1.5	0.2	0.1	0.1	0	0	1.9	4
Tourism	7.4	10.8	1.1	1.5	0.7	0.1	21.7	46
Service	0.6	0	0	0	0	0	0.7	2
Work	3.8	6.6	0.9	0.3	0.2	0.2	12.0	26
Other/ no information	0.5	0.4	0.3	0.1	0	0	1.5	3
Total	18.9	20.3	3.6	2.4	1.1	0.4	46.8	100
%	40	43	8	5	2	1	100	

A comparison of the means of transport used in 1978 and 1994 shows that there has been a decrease in the use of the car for long-distance journeys and a corresponding increase in air transport, measured in travel frequency (Frändberg 1996, p. 29).

In the light of this discussion on the effects of travel, a number of questions spring to mind: first at a general level, how can we organize our society differently so that while still maintaining a high level of welfare, we can reduce the level and frequency of mobility at least as regards the long distances? This also means that major changes in attitudes and lifestyles are necessary. Second, we may ask at the specific level whether it is possible to develop alternative forms of tourism and leisure activities that, at least in part, are located close to large population centres, which would lead to a reduction in travel, use of resources, and emissions of pollutants. Finally, how can we develop alternative forms of transport that would result in more sustainable development than is the case today?

ENERGY ASPECTS, ENVIRONMENTAL IMPACTS AND COSTS

General Comments on Energy Aspects of Mobility

The production of energy results in various kinds of environmental problems. The use of fossil fuel, e.g. oil, means that we are using the earth's finite resources and producing emissions through combustion. The production of electricity by means of water power entails local and regional encroachment on the natural and cultural landscape, both in the construction of dams and in transmission to the users. The use of nuclear energy for the production of electricity involves the risk of uncontrollable accidents and the problem of what to do with the radioactive waste.

The total consumption of energy in Sweden in 1988 was roughly distributed as follows. Industry, and households and services accounted for about 40% each and transport for about 20%. The amount of energy used in the transport sector is just under 90 terawatt hours (TWh). About 97% of this consists of the combustion of fossil fuels, i.e. petrol and diesel oil. Road traffic accounts for just over 70% and air transport and shipping for just over 10% each. Transport's relative share of oil consumption has increased in recent years, which is partly explained by the decrease in other sectors and partly by the increase, in absolute figures, in the transport sector (Miljödepartementet 1991, p. 220).

As is apparent from Table 7.3, the total consumption of energy for transport in Sweden increased over the period 1970–87. In absolute terms it is the private car that accounts for the clearly predominant consumption of energy whereas in relative terms, air transport accounts for the highest consumption per person-kilometre, followed by the car. Rail traffic has the lowest figure, measured in both relative and absolute terms.

Table 7.3. The consumption of energy for different forms of transport in Sweden, 1970–87. (MJ = megajoule. 1 MJ = 0.277 kiloWatt hours. PJ = petajoule. 1 PJ = 1 billion MJ). *Source*: Miljödepartementet (1991, p. 240).

Form of transport	Use of energy PJ		MJ/person-kilometres	
	1970	1987	1970	1987
Cars	108	159	1.95	2.02
Buses	5	9	0.92	1.03
Railways	3	4	0.50	0.52
Aircraft	4	9	6.11	3.13

Table 7.4. The primary energy consumption per person and kilometre for various forms of transport and various levels of capacity utilization. The estimates are based on an energy consumption over a distance of 2500 kilometres for land transport and 1950 kilometres for air transport. *Source*: Müller (1992).

Form of transport	Energy consumption Megajoule (MJ)
Trains	0.34
Tour buses	0.35
Private cars (4 people)	0.72
Private cars (3 people)	0.96
Private cars (2 people)	1.44
Private cars (1 person)	2.88
Aircraft (direct flights)	1.85

Examples of Energy Estimates for Tourism Transport

It is important to distinguish between tourism products where the demand is limited to the local environment and products which involve long-distance travel. One of the problems of long-distance tourism travel is the high energy consumption per person. In most cases, high energy consumption entails a high level of pollution.

Müller has attempted to calculate the consumption of energy per person and kilometre for various forms of transport for tourism travel (Müller 1992). The object of the exercise is twofold: to enable product developers to measure and evaluate a major environmental aspect of their products and to give the growing number of people who want to plan their holiday trips on an ecological basis a chance of choosing the least energy-intensive form of transport. Müller bases his calculations on the following assumptions.

> This strikes us as reasonable in that, as a general rule, transport accounts for up to 95 percent of all tour holiday energy requirements, depending on the distance involved. The remaining percentage goes on accommodation, food and leisure activities where energy requirements in terms of the whole are so negligible that surveying them would not be worthwhile. (Müller 1992)

According to the above quotation, 95 per cent of the energy requirements for tourism travel are for transport.[28] The remaining 5% of the energy is used in accommodation, activities etc. Unfortunately, Müller does not substantiate his assumption that transport accounts for as much as 95% of tour holiday energy consumption, which makes it difficult to verify. There is also a problem of delimitation in the calculation of energy requirements. Does it include, for instance, the construction of an accommodation amenity and the manufacture of leisure articles? The answer is probably 'No'. Müller's figures are given in Table 7.4 above.

> For energy audit purposes, we assumed confirmed occupancy averages of 60 percent for trains, 65 percent for scheduled flights, 85 percent for tour buses and 90 percent for charter flights and deducted the amount of energy consumed by freight transport on scheduled flights. (Müller 1992)

Without making our own calculations, it is difficult either to confirm or reject Müller's assumptions. However, the figures are interesting in that they attempt to analyse the consumption of energy in connection with tourism travel. What Müller does not include in his calculations is the fact that air transport in particular, but also rail, requires connecting transport to the airport or station, which increases the level of consumption. Further, we also need to take into account the fact that different forms of transport are run on different forms of energy coming from different sources and with different impacts on the environment.

Based on the survey of travel habits from 1994 and a number of assumptions, Frändberg (1996, pp. 49–53) calculates the consumption of energy and the emissions of certain air pollutants. Her material is presented in terms of the consumption of energy in relation to both the form of transport and the purpose of the journey. The estimated total consumption of energy in 1994 for long-distance journeys was 20 TWh, which is a third of the total energy used, 60 TWh, for the transportation of people in Sweden. International air transport represents 8% of the long-distance journeys but, on these journeys, it accounts for 55% of the energy requirements (see Table 7.5).

Table 7.5. Swedish people's long-distance travel classified according to form of transport, number of journeys, distance and energy consumption, 1994. *Source*: Frändberg (1996, p. 50). *TWh (terrawatt hour = one million million watt hours)

Form of transport	Journeys millions	%	Distance billions of kilometres	%	Energy TWh*	%
Car	43.5	70	18.9	40	7.4	36
Air	5.3	8	20.3	43	11.3	55
Train	5.6	9	3.6	8	0.5	3
Bus	4.2	7	2.4	5	0.3	2
Ship	1.4	2	1.1	2	0.7	4
Other/ no information	2.4	4	0.5	1	–	–
Total	62.4	100	46.8	100	20.1	100

According to Frändberg, long-distance tourism travel requires on average about the same amount of energy as long-distance travel to work. Thus, tourism travel does not use more energy-intensive forms of transport than travel to work. The high level of energy consumption given for tourism travel in Table 7.6 is then merely a result of the fact that the tourism journeys are comparatively long. The long tourism journeys (over 3000 km) represent about 10 per cent of the number of journeys and 50 per cent of the distance travelled and account for as much as 60 per cent of the energy consumption for tourism travel.

Table 7.6. Swedish people's long-distance travel classified according to purpose of journey, number of journeys, distance and energy consumption, 1994. *Source*: Frändberg (1996, p. 50).

Purpose of journey	Journeys millions	%	Distance billions of kilometres	%	Energy TWh	%
Tourism	18.9	30	21.7	46	9.1	45
Visit to relatives/friends	14.5	23	9.1	19	3.8	19
Work	15.3	25	12.0	26	5.7	28
Other	13.6	22	4.0	9	1.5	8
Total	62.3	100	46.8	100	20.1	100

SJ's (the National Swedish Railways) Environmental Computer Program

Statens Järnvägar (SJ) have developed a computer program which makes it easy to compare the emission of pollutants from various forms of transport, their consumption of energy and the environmental cost for a number of selected routes (SJ stab Information). The user can select either passenger or goods transport. For passenger transport there is a comparison between cars, buses, aircraft and trains, and for goods transport, between lorries, boats, aircraft and trains. The pollutants that are shown are hydrocarbons (HC), carbon monoxide (CO), nitrogen oxides (NOx) and carbon dioxide (CO_2). Hydrocarbons and carbon monoxide create problems at the local level, nitrogen oxides cause acidification and are a regional problem and carbon dioxide, which contributes to the greenhouse effect, creates global environmental problems.

Emissions are measured in kilos/person, the consumption of energy in kiloWatt hours (kWh) and the environmental costs in Swedish crowns (SEK). The environmental costs are based on the 'price tags' which the Swedish parliament has placed on different types of emission and which are used in policy making to evaluate, in economic terms, the costs to society of various emissions. Damage to nature entails a cost which is measurable in several ways, e.g. by calculating what it would cost to repair the damage. The environmental computer program has used the political planners' evaluation and this produces the following price list for the commonest emissions: carbon monoxide SEK 16/kg, hydrocarbons SEK 17/kg, nitrogen oxides SEK 43/kg, sulphur dioxide SEK 16/kg and carbon dioxide SEK 0.38/kg.

There are subheadings for each form of transport which may be selected when making comparisons; these include capacity utilization, whether or not the car has a catalytic converter, whether or not ethanol is used as bus fuel, the type of aircraft, and connecting journeys to airports. Variables which have not been included in the program relate to such matters as weather conditions, the driver's driving technique, and the vehicle's service requirements. The figures on which the program is based have been derived from survey and research reports. It is difficult to penetrate the serious scientific approach the report exudes without examining in detail the material that underpins it.[29]

It has been our ambition in producing the environmental computer program to provide an objective and clear picture of the average environmental impacts of your choice of transport. The program clarifies the relationship between the different forms of transport. The results should be seen as differences in size rather than as exact values. (SJ stab Information, p. 4, my translation)

In Tables 7.7 and 7.8 the program is used simply to provide examples in the form of comparisons between different forms of transport for a given journey and thus for the simulation of the impact on the environment. The examples in both tables indicate the environmental impacts etc. of a journey between the cities of Karlstad and Stockholm in Sweden. The distance by road is 313 kilometres, by air 306 and by rail 329. Table 7.7 compares a car with catalyst emission control and only one passenger (the driver), a diesel-powered bus with 50% capacity utilization, an aircraft of the type Fokker F28, which is currently used on the Karlstad–Stockholm route, with 65% capacity utilization, and a high-speed train of the type X2000, which again is currently in use between Karlstad and Stockholm, with 50% capacity utilization. The difference between the tables is that in Table 7.8 the capacity utilization for the car has been raised to four passengers, for the bus to 80%, for the aircraft to 100% and for the train to 75%. The other points of comparison are the same.

The example in Table 7.7 shows that, as regards impact on the environment, buses have the highest values for the emission of hydrocarbons, cars for the emission of carbon monoxide, and aircraft for the emission of nitrogen oxides and carbon dioxide. Aircraft also have the highest energy requirements and environmental costs. Trains have the best results in all categories.

Table 7.7. Differences between various forms of transport with low capacity utilization, indicated in the form of environmental impacts, energy consumption and environmental costs on the Karlstad–Stockholm route, according to SJ's environmental computer program.

Environmental impacts etc.	Form of transport			
	Private car catalyst converter, 1 passenger	Bus diesel-fuel 50% util.	Aircraft Fokker F28 65% util.	Train X2000 50% util.
Emissions (kg/person)				
HC (health risks)	0.01	0.03	0.02	0.00
CO (health risks)	0.15	0.03	0.08	0.00
NOx (acidification)	0.05	0.18	0.23	0.00
CO_2 (greenhouse effect)	53.84	10.64	63.80	0.54
Energy consumption (kWh)	200	41	248	26
Environmental costs (SEK)	22.49	11.73	31.52	0.23

The corresponding figures in Table 7.8, where a higher capacity utilization has been indicated throughout, show more or less the same results for the various forms of transport. However, the values for the car show a considerable improvement when compared with the low capacity utilization, which underlines the importance of car-pooling.

Table 7.8. Differences between different forms of transport with high capacity utilization, indicated in the form of environmental impacts, energy consumption and environmental costs on the Karlstad–Stockholm route, according to SJ's environmental computer program.

Environmental impacts etc	Form of transport			
	Private car catalyst converter, 4 passengers	Bus diesel-fuel 80% util.	Aircraft Fokker F28 100% util.	Train X2000 75% util.
Emissions (kg/person)				
HC (health risks)	0.00	0.02	0.01	0.00
CO (health risks)	0.04	0.02	0.05	0.00
NOx (acidification)	0.01	0.12	0.15	0.00
CO_2 (greenhouse effect)	13.46	6.89	41.31	0.36
Energy consumption (kWh)	50	25	161	16
Environmental costs SEK)	5.62	7.59	20.50	0.15

CONCLUDING REMARKS

The purpose of this section has been to show the relation between lifestyle, leisure activities and mobility in the population of contemporary Sweden and the environmental impacts of the high level of mobility. In many respects the discussion is valid for most countries in the rich world. I have shown how mobile various groups of the population are during their leisure, which leisure activities require mobility, and which forms of transport are used. Since different forms of transport require differing resource levels, e.g. in the form of fuel and land, consume varying amounts of energy and have different impacts on the environment, e.g. emissions and noise, the study provides a basis for an assessment of the further consequences of our mobility in connection with leisure activities. The presentation of the mobility and leisure activities of different population groups enables us to outline the characteristic features of a person who is active at or near home and one who is active far from home. People who are active at or near home and are thus not very mobile are, in some sense, a disadvantaged group whilst the opposite is true of highly mobile people who are active far from home. It is the people who are not particularly mobile during their leisure activities who are the most eco-friendly group.

The high level of mobility is closely related to the level of economic development in modern and late modern society. Two factors, in particular, create the conditions for high mobility: the globally specialized division of labour with a high level of transport of goods and people, and the spatial organization of society with its extensive division of functions. From the standpoint of distribution, the high level of mobility in the rich world contrasts strongly with the lack of mobility in the poor world.

Air pollution is one of the most serious environmental consequences, locally, regionally and globally, of transport and, in particular, road traffic. In road traffic it is the private car that produces the highest emission levels. Even the growing noise levels in society are primarily a result of road traffic. The latter also produces the highest continuous noise levels. Local noise problems, in some cases major ones, arise in connection with air and rail traffic. The highly mobile society in which we live today involves an extensive consumption of space for the infrastructure that is a precondition for our mobility. The infrastructure of the transport system affects both the urban and rural landscape and produces, among other things, barrier effects: areas that may be difficult for people and animals to cross.

The consequences of the use of the various forms of transport for tourism travel correspond well with the general picture we have given of the effects of the transport system. Our material shows that car and air tourism journeys are of major importance in a discussion of mobility and environmental impacts. We must distinguish here between tourism and leisure activities where the demand is limited to the local environment and those activities involving long-distance travel. One of the problems of long-distance tourism travel is the high level of energy consumption per person it entails. A high level of energy consumption generally means a high level of pollution. One conclusion that may be drawn from this is that to achieve environmentally sustainable development in tourism travel, we must either use other forms of transport than those that predominate today or travel shorter distances and, to a greater extent, take our holidays and pursue other leisure activities in the local environment. What is perhaps desirable from an environmental standpoint is a combination of forms of transport which produces both a good range and a certain flexibility. One example is (high-speed) trains and cycles.

PART 4

The Destination

CHAPTER 8

Sustainable Tourism Development at the Destination

INTRODUCTION

Up to this point my analysis has been based on the following model: the lifestyle of the tourist – tourism and leisure travel – impacts at the destination. One of the main issues I have considered is how to design a lifestyle analysis that will relate our present-day impact on the environment to mobility in the leisure area. In this chapter the perspective will be changed to an analysis of sustainable tourism development at the destination. When considered from this perspective, sustainability has a somewhat different content. The focus is still on environmental aspects, but the concept is broadened to include a survey both of the process of tourism production and its theoretical prerequisites and of the impacts of tourism on the destination which are of importance for sustainability in tourism development. The analysis of the local and regional consequences of tourism focuses on tourism in rural areas of Sweden. At the same time the results may be generalized for many countries and regions in Western Europe and North America. Finally, there is a section on regional planning for sustainable tourism development. This is based on a case-study of the work carried out of significant actors to achieve sustainable development and sustainable tourism development in the Värmland region in Sweden.

GENERAL COMMENTS ON TOURISM DEVELOPMENT

Butler (1980) (cf. Keller 1984) devised a hypothetical model for the development of tourism at destinations, which has resulted in a considerable number of further

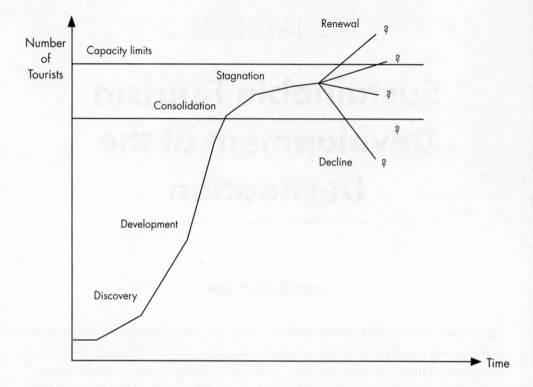

Figure 8.1. Hypothetical model for development at tourist destinations. *Source*: Butler (1980)

studies and discussion (see Figure 8.1). The model is basically a normal product cycle curve but what distinguishes it from other such curves is that it is applied to the development of tourism in places. In the model the vertical axis indicates the volume of tourists and the horizontal axis, time. The model shows that when a place and its attractions are first introduced in a market, there are few visitors. Gradually, people discover the area and the stream of tourists increases considerably. After this initial phase, there is a period of maturity and stagnation. If nothing is done about the situation, for instance, the introduction of new tourism products, there is a decline in visitor frequency. These arguments apply primarily to areas which have good preconditions for (mass) tourism. Further, the tourism products and other services are adapted to a certain level of tourism and this sets the capacity limits. If the number of visitors is under this level, it might be necessary to discontinue or change the product; if it is above, capacity must be increased. There is also an upper limit to what the area can sustain, i.e. the limit of its 'carrying capacity' (cf. Eadington and Eadington 1986; Wallsten 1988).

The model illustrates the time aspect of tourism development very clearly.

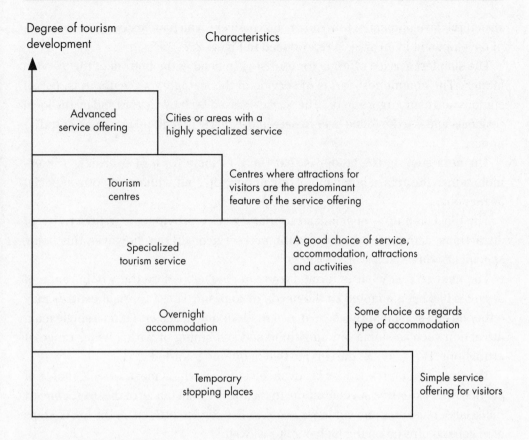

Figure 8.2. Development of a specialized offering for tourists. *Source*: Flognfeldt and Onshus (1996, p. 12)

However, it has been criticized as too deterministic and not taking into account that places are unique. One simple interpretation of the model as regards sustainable tourism development would be to attempt to keep tourism in a particular place within the limits of the capacity of the place. However, there are many different forms of tourism which can produce effects that are more or less sustainable. One exciting question is how the new differentiated and, in some cases, small-scale forms of tourism fit into Butler's model. These late modern forms of tourism are based more on specialization, niche areas and high competence than on earning money from volume tourism. The model is not wholly adequate for analysing the development of these forms in an area except in those cases where the small-scale form of tourism opens up an area for mass tourism.

Butler's model of tourism development at the destination is, as I have noted, very general. A model which provides a more detailed picture of how to achieve the structural development of tourism or, alternatively, which indicates different levels of development in an area, is reproduced in Figure 8.2.

The simplest service offering for tourists is placed at the bottom of the 'service ladder'. The commonest forms of service in this category are cafeterias, petrol stations and hamburger stands. The service is used both by visitors and by the local residents and is to be found everywhere, particularly in built-up areas and at traffic nodes.

The next step up the ladder is that there is some form of overnight accommodation in the area, a hotel, motel or camping site, but without any other special attractions.

The third step up is specialized tourism service providing a greater range of attractions, activities, accommodation and service without, however, this being specifically directed towards visitors.

The next step is what is termed tourism centres, where the whole range of services has been adapted to the needs of tourism. These tourism centres may either be one-season or two-season destinations and based either on a single main attraction such as skiing or sunbathing and swimming or with a wider range of attractions. However, all the service that is offered is varied.

The final step on the ladder is advanced service, which means a rich choice of services and extensive specialization, in the form, for instance, of theatres, concert halls, large museums and congress centres. The service offered on the lower steps is in general offered on the higher steps as well.

It is easier to fit the late modern forms of tourism into this model (see Figure 8.2) than into Butler's. On an ecotourism trip the lower steps on the service ladder can be utilized for buying food, for instance. In contrast, the higher steps would be used for buying advanced leisure equipment. On educational trips, the advanced service that is requested might be in the form of museums in big cities. At the same time, the model may be seen as a stage in the development from small-scale tourism to mass tourism. In countries which have only a few of the conditions necessary for developing mass tourism their best chance lies primarily in building up unique and specialized products and in acquiring a high level of competence. I will consider this in the next section.

AN ANALYSIS OF TOURISM IN TERMS OF DEVELOPMENT STRATEGY AND PRODUCTION THEORY

When developing a destination, a planner works, on the one hand, with what are called 'pull factors', i.e. the planner concentrates on what can be done to develop and improve an area's tourism products and attractions for tourism. On the other hand, the work consists of determining the demand, i.e. the reasons why we travel or do not travel. When an existing and potential demand has been identified, information can be provided about the supply in an area and the attractions marketed; these are the so-called 'push factors'. An area's tourism products and attractions can be designed in structurally different ways and these can be underpinned by a development strategy. The idea of a development strategy is that it should provide the guidelines for planning a certain development. A strategy consists of visions and goals for the future and the means to achieve them. An applied development strategy in an area should deal with the following points and questions, most of which relate in some way to the sustainability aspects of tourism development.

• Inventory of existing and potential resources for tourism.
• Description and analysis of the structure of the tourist industry – the regional tourism product (cf. Kamfjord 1993).
• Analysis of the demand.
• Survey of the development ambitions of the representatives of the tourist industry.
• Survey of the wishes of the local residents regarding the development of tourism.
• How can both a good physical and ecological environment and a good social and cultural one be maintained when developing tourism?
• Where should the tourist industry be developed?
• When should the various parts of the tourist industry be developed?
• What level of tourism is desirable?
• Is it possible and desirable to lengthen the season?
• What form of organization for tourism issues should there be in the area in question?

The above description and analysis of tourism at the destination may be taken further. Tourism's production and consumption process can be described in terms of a simple model with four steps: resources and preconditions – products – marketing and distribution – demand and consumption (see Figure 8.3). There is also a fifth step which comprises the impact of tourism on an area, i.e. it includes the consequences of tourism. The model should be seen in the context of how tourism may be developed in an area. Moreover, the arguments primarily relate to resource-based leisure tourism and less to business travel and visits to relatives and friends. In its graphic design the model is static and its various parts should be analysed over a period of time, or alternatively in the form of comparable time sections, in order to achieve the process dimension. The parts of the model are

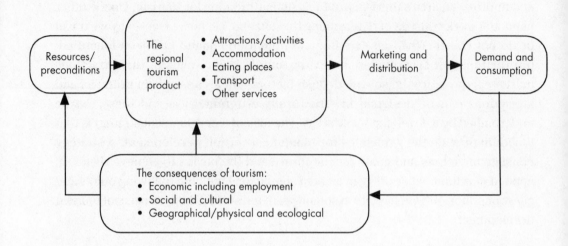

Figure 8.3. A model of the components in tourism's production and consumption process and the consequences of tourism.

differentiated only to a relatively small degree. A certain nuancing is achieved in the text but this could be further developed.

The first step, analysing the resources, can be performed by asking a number of questions. The following are some examples: What are the 'raw materials' for the production of tourism? What use is made of the resources and preconditions for the production of tourism?

Zimmermann (1972) has a broad definition of a resource as something which at a given point in time fulfils a function for people. A function generally has a purpose, e.g. satisfying a need. A resource may be seen as a means of achieving certain goals and it thereby reflects people's values. Zimmermann's definition implies that a resource is developed in a dynamic interplay between nature and culture. The sum of man's ability to benefit from experiences and knowledge and transmit them over time may be termed culture and it is thus culture that at a given point in time defines what resources are. According to Zimmermann's definition, there must be a (potential) demand before a resource can be utilized for production. At the same time, there is a whole set of restrictions which prevent a product from being consumed by everybody.

The resources for tourism can be divided into a number of categories such as natural conditions, e.g. climate or topographical conditions; cultural conditions, e.g. prehistoric remains, cultural landscape or cultural heritage; and resources which can be manipulated, e.g. the creation of synthetic attractions (Svalastog 1994,

p. 63). Even such things as the provision of knowledge and skills and the provision of capital are necessary for producing and implementing the tourism product. It is here that the content and orientation of the educational system, institutions providing capital, development institutes and authorities come in the picture. There is a definite need for entrepreneurs and enthusiasts into the production process. Besides the resources mentioned, tourism has to work with such preconditions as legal requirements.

The nature of the tourism industry may primarily be described as service production, which includes the core businesses in the industry, e.g. activities, accommodation and catering. However, the tourism industry is also dependent on the production of goods, which may be seen as peripheral businesses, e.g. material for building facilities or provisions for restaurants. The products, or the tourism industry, are usually divided into a number of sub-areas (see Figure 8.3). Regional tourism production is a generic term for describing the tourism industry in a region from a holistic perspective or as a composite industry made up of a number of separate components. Some of the questions that may help to illustrate the problems involved in analysing a product or destination are: How can the product mix at a destination be designed and developed? How are networks and 'packages' in a region constructed so as to achieve a holistic tourism product? What are the incentives for competition or cooperation in the tourism industry? How can tourism complement other commercial and industrial activity in a region?

Svalastog classifies products in two main groups (Svalastog 1996). The first group consists of standard products. This includes much of mass tourism, above all in the form of packaged holidays. The second group, which contains non-standard products, includes the following:

- 'Know-how' products, which require a high level of knowledge. Examples are advanced nature and culture guides.
- 'Special products', which may be based on special competence or on the fact that the raw material has special or unique conditions.
- 'Niche' products. Here a company has gained a competitive edge in a limited field, through, for instance, marketing. The product as such may be either standard or of the 'know-how' type.

Svalastog argues that it is primarily in the non-standard field that countries which lack the conditions for mass tourism have a good chance of developing tourism in the future and thus it is towards this area that society's organizations should direct their interest.

How can the public sector, in cooperation with the tourism industry, achieve an optimal investment in tourism in a particular area? The starting-point for this is a further question: Why do visitors come to the area? The simple answer is that there is, in the broadest sense, something attractive there. This leads us to draw the conclusion that the primary objective from the standpoint of society is to invest in tourist attractions and to create suitable infrastructural solutions. It is, namely, possible to argue that if a greater power of attraction creates a greater demand, there is also a market for tourism products in other sub-areas of the regional tourism product such as food, accommodation, transport and other services, which would then develop more or less automatically. In many regions in the Nordic countries the basic preconditions for tourism production are nature and culture. It is therefore important to support the development of a distinctive variety of attractions in the fields of nature and culture. There has been a focus on differentiated nature tourism in the development of tourism throughout the rich world since the mid-1980s. A new major trend that is emerging is the development of a range of products in the field of culture tourism (heritage products), which will thus be the equivalent of the differentiated forms of nature tourism. What is required, then, in the form of investments for a region to develop new products in the field of nature and culture? Apart from the basic prerequisite, entrepreneurs, what is needed is financial support to develop attractions. The public sector can also help by providing the necessary knowledge and competence. Further, the planner should adopt the perspective of the tourist and act as a facilitator in the process; providing easily comprehensible and good information about tourism products and the environment, making it easy for the tourist to book a journey and providing simple transport solutions, which, at the same time, cause least damage to the environment.

To go on to the other steps in the model (see Figure 8.3), marketing is carried out, on the one hand, directly by the tourism companies and, on the other, by regional and area tourist organizations. Distribution is in the hands of various tour operators such as travel agents and booking companies. A major issue here is how to provide an attractive picture of a tourism product or area which is fair, gives the right signals and creates the right level of expectation in the customer. This issue is not least important from the perspective of the environment.

Consumption or demand for tourism products can be classified in various ways. The fundamental change in society from the industrial to the post-industrial or late modern phase has already been discussed. One of the ways in which this change is noticeable is the increase in tourism products and travel. This process is thus fundamental in a discussion of changes in the consumption of tourism (Karlsson 1994, 1998). When it comes to tourism products, one often starts with the motive for the journey and designs some kind of segmentation. The following are some of the questions that may help to clarify an analysis of consumption and demand. What are the forces underpinning the consumption of and demand for tourism products and how do these change over time? How do underlying factors such as lifestyle, gender, age/life-cycle and home region affect consumption in tourism and leisure?

Tourism has various types of consequences in an area, the main categories being economic, social and cultural, and physical and ecological. These consequences affect both the resources and the conditions for tourism as well as the tourism product; they may have both a positive and a negative impact. We shall consider this impact below. As is apparent, a large number of questions have to be answered in order to create a basis for an analysis of tourism at a destination in terms of development strategy. When strategic documents are being drawn up for tourism development in a region, sustainability issues should permeate the whole analysis and not be limited to their own (isolated) section of the text.

THE IMPACT OF TOURISM WITH THE EMPHASIS ON CONDITIONS IN RURAL AREAS

General Comments

Tourism and leisure activities have various types of impact on a region (cf. Aronsson 1989, 1993, 1997; Gunn 1988; Krippendorf 1989; Lea 1988; Mathieson and Wall 1982; Murphy 1985; Pearce, D. 1981; Pearce, P. L. 1988). A general indication of the main types is given in Figure 8.4. Taken together, they determine how sustainable tourism is in a particular area.

We shall demonstrate some of the impacts of tourism in very general terms and primarily in relation to conditions in rural areas in Sweden (e.g., Aronsson 1989, pp. 129–203). The account may be seen as a set of indicators for sustainable tourism development in the local perspective. Initially it should be pointed out that the capacity of communities and areas to withstand the impacts of tourism depends on how robust they are in a number of respects. It may depend on the number and type of visitors but also on the economic diversity of the area, its social and cultural structure and its geographical, physical and ecological capacity. At the local level, sustainable tourism development is primarily a matter of preserving the resource base. Further, tourism must have long-term sustainability in a number of respects. Natural and cultural resources are central to the development of tourism. However, these resources are finite and this means they can be overexploited. Like many other industries, the tourism industry has a tendency to base its actions on short-term economic thinking. An unrestricted and unplanned development of tourism can lead to the deterioration or destruction of both natural and cultural conditions, ranging from disruptions to the ecosystem of an area to a negative impact on the cultural heritage.

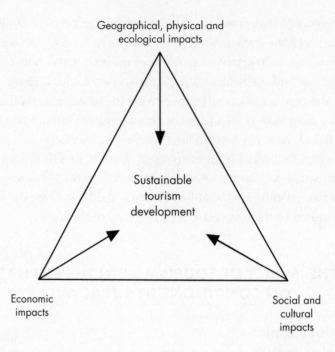

Geographical, physical and
ecological impacts

Sustainable
tourism
development

Economic
impacts

Social and
cultural
impacts

Figure 8.4. An illustration of some of the basic impacts of tourism in an area in relation to sustainable tourism development.

The production of tourism has socio-economic consequences; for instance, it increases the customer base or market for services such as food shops, it creates employment and it has revenue effects at municipal, county council and national levels. At the same time, it is seasonal and this means much part-time employment, capacity utilization problems for the retail trade and increased costs for the public sector for police, fire brigade, health care etc. Seen from the viewpoint of business economics, starting tourism companies would in general seem to be problematic, particularly during the first few years of activity in capital-intensive companies. In rural areas long-term economic effects can be best achieved if tourism is allowed to grow fairly slowly. This increases the opportunities for the tourism industry to become integrated with other local industry and thus create direct economic utility for the area. If tourism grows rapidly and on a large scale, the effect is often the opposite, in that companies come in from the outside and the economic leakage from the rural area to places with a greater supply of services is considerable. This reasoning implies that there is a difference between urban and rural areas. Another aspect of the economic dimension is the fact that a one-sided development of tourism in an area, as with other industrial activities, can have negative effects.

The ideal is, then, local industry which is characterized by diversity, where tourism is a complement in the economy.

One geographical aspect of the development of tourism in an area is that it leads to improvements in the infrastructure, which also benefits the local population and their opportunities for local recreation. With a significant contribution from tourist traffic, communications in an area may also be improved, for instance, more bus services and more frequent departures. Tourism may also have ecological and environmental impacts, both through changes in the landscape due to exploitation for infrastructure and tourist activities, and through damage, wear and tear, and litter as a result of the stream of tourists. Place-related problems mainly occur in connection with large-scale and high-frequency tourism, but even small-scale tourism can cause damage if the natural landscape is particularly sensitive. The general problem of transport in connection with tourism has been dealt with earlier. Wear and tear from tourism is a local problem and it should, in most cases, be possible to solve it through better planning and management. This type of damage should not be neglected but I would maintain that, compared to the damage and changes caused by forestry, the damage from tourism is minor. An interesting issue is the lively debate on the impact of tourism on the natural environment which is often conducted in the media in the Nordic countries. The intensity of this debate is probably due to two factors. The first is tradition. In comparison with forestry, tourism is a new industry and, as it is a service, it is different in kind from the primary industries. Second, to continue the comparison with forestry, land owners receive direct income from felling trees. As for tourism, it is generally other interests than land owners who receive the direct earnings. The indirect income from tourism, such as that for food, is not as visible.

Tourism also has social and cultural impacts (cf. Crouch 1994). These derive from the fact that a local community, including its culture and nature, is both the living environment for the local residents and 'raw material' for the tourism industry. The general tendency is for problems to arise when tourism becomes too large-scale and predominant in an area. The effect of this may be that people find it increasingly difficult to carry out their everyday tasks. Examples are crowded service establishments and full car parks (Aronsson 1993). Other examples of problems that may arise in tourist-intensive areas are an increase in drug abuse and crime. On the positive side, an area that has an attractive leisure environment gets good publicity. Many Swedish municipalities use their fine environment with opportunities for recreation and leisure as an enticement in job adverts and when trying to attract companies. The effect may be that companies move into the area, with more job opportunities as a result, or that the skill levels in a municipality are improved as key people move in.

A DIFFERENTIATED PICTURE OF THE IMPACTS OF TOURISM

Developing tourism in an area is seldom unproblematic. It is important for all parties, the tourists, the residents, the tourism industry and the public sector, to create locally adapted forms of tourism. How, then, can we achieve a form of tourism that is acceptable to them all? To give a complete and unambiguous answer to this question is virtually impossible. In order to gain local support when planning tourism in an area, it is essential to take certain conditions into consideration (Aronsson 1989, pp. 266–9). The perspective adopted, then, is that of the social planner. The importance of demand for the development of tourism must not be neglected and is implicit in the following discussion. As we mentioned above, the receiving area's economic, social and cultural structures, and natural conditions should be taken into account. These structures and conditions should determine the form of the tourism being planned. If the residents get what they consider a reasonable return on their investment, the acceptance level for tourism will probably be greater. Butler describes the conditions for tourism development in the following terms:

> Tourism is an industry, but it is also a form and agent of development and change and must be recognised as such. Controlled and managed properly, it can be a non- or low-consumptive utilizer of resources and can operate on a sustainable basis. However, if developed beyond the capacity of the environment, the resource base, and the local population to sustain it, it ceases to be a renewable resource industry and it instead becomes . . . a 'boom-bust enterprise'. (Butler 1992, p. 34)

Figure 8.5 presents a number of questions which are of great importance for adapting tourism to local conditions. These questions also provide a differentiated picture of the impacts of tourism at the local level.

How to achieve participation in the planning process?

Two key factors for adapting tourism to local conditions are the degree of local (political) control and the extent and level of planning. In the development of mass tourism, in particular, the tendency is for the local control which exists initially to lessen and be gradually transferred to external control. Similarly, the planning process generally changes from active to reactive as tourism develops into mass tourism (Butler 1992, p. 39).

The normative picture is different. A planning process involving as many as possible of those affected by the planning may be seen as a democratic issue and a matter of utilizing local resources in an appropriate manner. Most people have

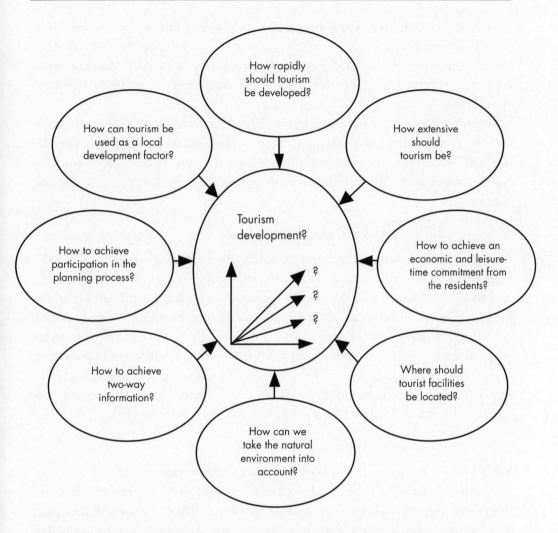

Figure 8.5. Important questions for the local adaptation of tourism development.

an interest in helping to form their local environment. The production of tourism entails an encounter between people, and an encounter on equal terms presupposes that the residents are involved from the planning stage onwards and that production is adapted to local conditions. In other words, it is a matter of making use of the power inherent in the population in an area in a manner which is constructive both for themselves and for the community (cf. Sveriges Turistråd 1991).

How can tourism be used as a local development factor?

The economies of destinations or host areas have two distinctive features: how advanced they are and the degree of leakage from them. With conventional tourism the economy of the area usually becomes more advanced as tourism expands, but there is always leakage from the area to economies with a greater supply of goods and services. In areas based, for instance, on wilderness tourism, the economies are generally very simple with a high degree of leakage, which reduces the exchange (Butler 1992, p. 39).

Tourism which is planned so that it primarily utilizes area-based resources creates local economic utility, provides employment for the inhabitants of the area, benefits the local service structure and achieves the highest degree of acceptance from the resident population. This may also be expressed as an increase in the social carrying capacity.

How rapidly should tourism be developed?

A society survives through the continuity of its culture, among other things. A 'new' industry like tourism affects the social network: people might change jobs, or more and new people move into the area. A change of this nature can be a shot in the arm for a district. At the same time, particularly in a situation of rapid change, conflicts may arise between people who are rooted in the new and old industries respectively or in different value systems. A slow rate of development for tourism is preferable; this makes it possible to overview the situation and provides a better opportunity for preventing problems. In general, a suitable rate of development is one where tourism is integrated socially and culturally into the area.

How extensive should tourism be?

What is a suitable number of tourists in an area? It is impossible to give a general answer to this question. Each area has its own specific level of tolerance with regard to tourists. As a general comment, however, we can say that if tourism is well adapted to the local community, the level of tolerance is raised. We can also make a distinction between large urban areas and rural areas. In rural areas and in smaller places tourists easily become a dominant feature with the result that crowding and conflicts may occur. Further, if tourism is developed to such an extent that it results in a one-sided industrial structure, this will lead to greater economic vulnerability in an area.

There is also a difference between the various forms of tourism. In the short term, the new differentiated and small-scale forms of tourism result in smaller changes at the destination than conventional large-scale tourism. This is in part due to the fact that they require smaller and fewer facilities. In the longer term, however, the specialized forms of tourism may result in greater and more far-reaching changes. Contacts between tourists and residents and the effects of these contacts are one example where there is a danger of the specialized forms encroaching on the personal space of the residents to a greater extent than conventional tourism.

Carrying capacity is an instrument for regulating the number of visitors. Another way of influencing the size of tourism is to concentrate marketing on specific segments. Local and regional planners should also reach a decision about the spatial spread or concentration of tourism and whether it should develop horizontally through the establishment of several small companies or vertically through the growth of an individual company (de Kadt 1992, pp. 58–9).

How to achieve an economic and leisure-time commitment from the residents?

If jobs are created in tourism for as many groups of the resident population as possible and the tourist activities can also be enjoyed by the local population, this will lead to greater tolerance of tourism in an area. Further, it is important to maintain or strengthen the social networks at a destination. This can be achieved by economically and physically planning the rate of expansion so that the social network has time to develop. It can also be achieved by establishing meeting points between residents and tourists.

Raising the level of knowledge and formal competence in the tourism industry through education is a further aspect that needs to be considered. This is particularly necessary where unique tourism products are involved. Moreover, if the idea is to employ a large proportion of local labour in specialized tourism products, the resident population must also have a chance of education.

Where should tourist facilities be located?

Facilities and other permanent amenities for tourism and leisure activities should be located so that they do not hinder public access to the countryside. Further, facilities should complement one another and, if possible, make use of a common infrastructure. Furthermore, the location of facilities should be planned together with other sectoral interests to avoid conflicts over the use of land etc. One of the predominant factors of change in the landscape in connection with tourism development is infrastructural expansion for the transport system. This expansion often entails greater encroachment on the natural environment than the damage caused by the tourists themselves.

How can the natural environment be taken into account?

The impact of tourism on the natural environment is, in the main, dependent on the amount of tourism and the sensitivity of an area. Large-scale tourism, particularly in its early stages, often exerts considerable pressure on sensitive and unique areas. With the new small-scale forms of tourism, particularly in the long term, there is even more pronounced pressure on the unique and most sensitive areas. The reason is that alternative tourists seek out these areas (Butler 1992, pp. 38–9).

When planning for tourism, it is essential to take the carrying capacity of the environment into consideration and channel the tourists to those natural sites that are more resistant to wear and tear. Further, larger facilities for waste disposal are needed. Educating tourists and getting them to show consideration is a major factor in reducing the damage they cause to nature. Competent planning and management measures will also help to minimize the damage to nature.

How to achieve two-way information?

If the purpose of tourism development is to avoid a confrontation between tourists and residents and to provide residents with a reasonable chance of being involved in the tourism industry, then information and knowledge are essential. On the one hand, the tourists should be given comprehensive information about the host community and, on the other, the residents should be given information and have an opportunity to learn about the problems and possibilities of tourism.

Further Consideration of the Ecological Impacts of Tourism and the Flow of Materials

Frändberg (1993, pp. 9–35) has made a study of the consumption of resources, consumer patterns and lifestyle in connection with tourism. The study area, Koster, in Strömstad municipality on the west coast of Sweden was chosen because it consisted of islands, which form a naturally delimited area, and it is possible to identify all major transportation to and from the area. Moreover, large numbers of tourists visit the area during the summer months. Frändberg's study attempted to answer the question of how the flows of materials initiated by people to, from and within Koster vary with the tourist season (*ibid.*, p. 9). The study focuses on the material flows in space resulting from tourism travel. This distinguishes it from economic surveys which deal with the flow of money resulting from tourism and exclude the consequences of material flows, stressing the fact that the tourism product is an immaterial service produced and consumed in the same place and at the same time. Or, as Frändberg puts it: 'The changes in the flows of materials corresponding to the additional turnover are, however, seldom the subject of reflection or interest in studies focusing on the economic effects' (*ibid.*, p. 29, my translation).

The majority of studies dealing with the negative environmental impacts of tourism underline the fact that these are due to the tourists' lack of knowledge, or to poor planning, in that tourists are channelled to the wrong places. People's movements in space are seen then, in one sense, as separate from the resource base. Frändberg's study highlights tourism as an extensive mover of people but also of goods, which makes it extremely interesting. One way of studying the flow of materials which is discussed in the report is to follow the life-cycle of resource utilization, or, to use a time-geographical expression, to follow a trajectory, which means following a product or a subject through its various stages of transformation. This approach helps to provide a kind of holistic perspective on the problem in time and space, from resource to waste, alternatively from resource to recycling. Another approach is to delimit a geographical area, i.e. a more place-related than product-related approach. With this approach it is not possible to follow the flow of material in all its stages. Frändberg has chosen the latter approach in her study of tourism on Koster.

> The geographical delimitation should be seen as part of the issue itself, which concerns the flow of materials to Koster, a flow which varies over time. The geographical delimitation has as its objective to make visible the material relation of the community of Koster to its surroundings, and in this case how tourism affects it. (Frändberg 1993, p. 10, my translation)

Even this approach means that time and space are of central importance. A picture of how the total flow of goods varied over the year was gained from a study of the invoices from the major freight company. The months of February and July were selected as they represent the low and high seasons. Since the supply of goods in an ordinary foodstore is considerable, a particular group of products, detergents for washing, washing-up and cleaning, was chosen for special study. This group was selected because they are everyday articles and because tourism probably has a strong impact on the size of the flow. They were also chosen because of their contents, i.e. they include components that have a negative impact on the environment. In brief, the study showed that the consumer pattern on Koster changed from February, a month which may be considered to be free of any tourist impact, to July, when tourism has a major impact. Transport and the flow of goods was much more extensive in July and also of a partially different character, primarily because of the considerable increase in drinks. Further, the volume of waste was nearly twenty times larger in July than in February. As regards the special study, the flow of washing detergents showed no variation between winter and summer, which might be due to the fact that many tourists stay for a week or less and take their washing home with them. On the other hand, the consumption of detergents for washing-up and cleaning showed a very clear seasonal variation. Frändberg even considers the seasonal variation in individual substances in detergents which affect the environment. Most of these show an increase during the summer period and this can probably be ascribed to tourism. Frändberg draws

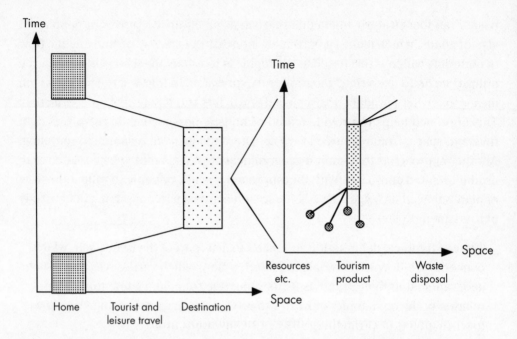

Figure 8.6. A time-geographical illustration of a tourist journey and the life-cycle of a tourism product.

Table 8.1. A property space for different forms of tourism.
Source: Karlsson (1994, p. 31).

	Centre	**Periphery**
Education and self-development	Mainly culture tourism, so-called highbrow cultural activities, e.g. visits to the theatre, museums and art galleries	Culture tourism as in the centre but more oriented towards the 'cultural heritage', e.g. visits to homestead museums and homestead weeks
Carnival	Strolling	Nature tourism
	Shopping	Seaside tourism
	Enjoying oneself, e.g. going to a restaurant or amusement park	Mountain tourism
		Visiting a theme park and similar places

the general conclusion that the lifestyle and consumer patterns of tourists 'generate much more waste than the lives the residents live' (*ibid.*, p. 21).

Frändberg's study provides a relatively good illustration of the reasoning to be found in time-geographical studies of material flows (cf. Lenntorp 1993). However, as we mentioned earlier, there are a number of different methods that may be used for determining the direction and delimitation of studies of material flows, including the choice of study unit. Part of this reasoning is given a time-geographical illustration in Figure 8.6.

The various methods of studying material flows may be classified as follows:

- Article level, e.g. 'tracing' the life-cycle of a tent.
- Object level, e.g. studying a tourism activity and the necessary resources and conditions for setting up and running the activity.
- Area level, e.g. studying material flows for a sample of tourism activities or products in a delimited geographical unit.
- Consumer level, i.e. 'following' the tourist through the various stages of a journey from planning prior to the journey to evaluation after returning home, and studying his or her consumption, the resource requirements during the journey, and waste disposal. A tourist journey may be said to consist of five different phases: (a) the planning period prior to departure, (b) the journey to the destination, (c) the stay at the destination, (d) the journey home and (e) evaluation after returning home.

A Differentiated Picture of the Cultural Impact of Tourism, and Authentic and Synthetic Tourism Products

The reasons for seeking the non-everyday or a time–space other than the everyday vary from person to person and range from the search for pleasure, entertainment or an escape from the everyday to the desire for education and self-development. Karlsson (1994) terms the former type of travel carnival and the latter education and self-development. The motives people have for travelling are satisfied in different spatial arenas ranging from the economic and political centre of society (the city) to its periphery (the countryside). Karlsson's division of tourism leads to the following property space for different forms of tourism (see Table 8.1).

One question concerning Karlsson's property space is where to place the specialized forms of tourism such as adventure and wilderness tourism. It is not completely self-evident that they fit into the category of education and self-development in the periphery. One way of capturing this new and growing form of tourism is to use Cohen's (1972) classification of tourism on a scale ranging from organized mass tourism to individual tourism of an explorative nature. This classification has a number of interesting dimensions for our purposes. With collectively organized mass tourism, the tourist is often in his or her own environmental sphere even at the destination, i.e. this dimension contains a large element of security throughout the journey. The unorganized individual tourist, on the other hand, seeks adventure or a degree of insecurity. These dimensions complement Karlsson's property space (see Table 8.2). It should be added that Karlsson's educational category is often individual whilst carnival travel is generally organized on a collective basis.

Table 8.2. A complementary property space for different forms of tourism.

	Sense of security	Sense of insecurity
Collective travel	Mass tourism	Adventure and ecotourism in groups
Individual travel	To known and (safe) places	'Exploring' unknown places

Table 8.3. A rough classification of the destination/tourism product in a property space.

Qualities of the destination tourism product	The main feature of the destination/tourism product	
	Nature	Culture
Authentic	A relatively unaltered landscape for tourism	A relatively unaltered social environment/ object for tourism
Synthetic	A landscape designed for tourism	A social environment/ object designed for tourism

The classifications presented above can be seen as a way of creating a differentiated picture of what the tourist demands. Whilst, on the one hand, showing the links between different groups of tourists, they also reveal the relationship of aspects of late modern forms of tourism to other tourism. The forms of tourism that are generally termed sustainable are to be found in the small-scale categories.

Let us return to the question of the two main motives for travel suggested by Karlsson (1994), carnival and education. Which of these two is the innate driving force for travel is of major importance for the development of the tourism product at the destination. Is the carnival motive a sign that we are really seeking a break from a monotonous and routinized everyday life? Roughly speaking, the earlier presentation of the leisure activities of the Swedish people indicated that blue-collar workers travel differently from white-collar ones. Does the carnival motive in general result in us seeking synthetic tourism products? Does the educational motive, on the other hand, mean that, on the whole, we already have satisfying work, satisfactory housing and so on and that we are primarily seeking authentic tourism products? Naturally, human existence is extremely complex, as are motives, but the core of mass tourism, for example, is probably pleasure and escape, i.e. carnival before education.

Synthetic tourism products are those whose purpose is to stimulate socially created commercial needs. Theme parks are typical examples of this category. Authentic tourism products, on the other hand, focus on the tourists' subjective experience of authenticity, genuineness and the untouched aspects of the nature and culture of an area. From the perspective of the host area and its population, it is of crucial importance whether the area, including its tourism products, maintains its authenticity or whether synthetic tourism products are created (Aronsson 1994, 1997).

If we leave the motive for travel, which in itself results in various types of tourism travel, and instead consider the destination and tourism product, we may draw up the rough classification in Table 8.3.

The concepts of nature and culture, on the one hand, and authentic and synthetic, on the other, are relative. This means that we can ask such questions as: Where can we find an untouched natural landscape? Most landscapes have at some time been altered by human activities and could therefore be considered as cultural landscapes. Here we use the term in its broad sense, i.e. a landscape which has been affected by the totality of human life and activities in society. Further, in this context, authenticity is synonymous with genuineness, a subjective experience and a question of degree. Everything may be said to be authentic at some point in time. Following this line of reasoning, the synthetic, the artificial, thus becomes more authentic with time. As long as one is aware of the relative nature of the concepts, I would maintain that they are useful in the development of tourism. In Table 8.3 the concepts should be understood as referring to landscapes and environments which are either unaffected by or are designed for tourism (cf. Buttimer 1978; MacCanell 1989; Malmberg 1980; Relph 1976; Ringer 1998; Sack 1986; Selwyn 1996).

The development of a tourist infrastructure and tourism products can be seen as an expression of the way the economic system works in creating a supply where there is a growing demand, which may be described as the process of commodification. It is often claimed that tourism results in nature, culture and relations being commodified. Even if this is the result of tourism, it is at the same time the result of the larger process of development in society. MacCanell was one of the first to analyse the commodification of tourism. To become an attraction, an object must be christened and given a name and thereby associated with a symbol or marker which makes it recognizable for the visitor and turns it into something special that is worth seeing (cf. Blom 1994). Before an object can be shown, it must be prepared, framed in some way and marked so that is distinguishable from other objects. Once it is separated from the ordinary world, it becomes sacred in the ritual of tourism. The former meaning of the object is removed and replaced by a new one in the tourism system. Marked in this way, it designates the identity of a community for the visitor (Lanfant and Graburn 1992, p. 100; MacCanell 1989).

The emphasis on the natural landscape in Sweden as one of the last major wildernesses in Europe is a significant feature in marketing the country abroad. A problem for commercial interests in tourism is how to earn money from nature since it is freely available to all – in Sweden we have the so-called 'every man's right', which means free access to nature. The answer is simple but difficult to achieve: turn nature into product. One question that arises here is to what extent nature can be commercialized and turned into a product. Countries like Sweden probably have considerable scope for new forms of tourism in the natural and cultural fields. An important planning tool is to be able to restrict the number of simultaneous visitors. The question remains, however, how we can preserve the innate significance of, for instance, a cultural object.

Many rural areas in Sweden have so far offered tourists very similar products. For example, the profile has very much been gatherings of folk musicians and handicraft. It is a challenge to the Swedish tourism industry to create diversity, to develop products with a high degree of uniqueness, or to develop the level of knowledge and skill in the tourism product.

The tourist attractions and the provision of activities do not just consist of stationary facilities and permanent sights but also of temporary events. There is a degree of authenticity and artificiality throughout the whole chain of offerings for tourists. One way of classifying the provision of tourism in a place which is of importance for the discussion on sustainability is in a property space constructed of some of the factors considered below (see Table 8.4). When the tourist travels from home to one or more destinations, an encounter takes place with the local residents and environment (Aronsson 1993, 1997; Krippendorf 1989). This encounter can be designated as a meeting place which may have a number of different features. One consequence of the structure of what is offered is the sense either of place identity or of placelessness and this is a distinction that is of importance for both the resident and the tourist.

In authentic meeting places the encounter generally takes place on the residents' terms. From a social and cultural perspective, the authentic meeting place can be characterized as a sustainable tourism product in itself as long as it is not altered to any significant extent by tourism. The critical factors for sustainability are therefore the number of visitors and the extent to which the tourism form encroaches on the local living environment. At the same time, even the authentic tourism products have a commercial peripheral organization which is not without significance in this context. The authentic meeting place is very sensitive to exploitation for tourism and to a growing demand from tourists.

MacCanell (1989) maintains that peripheral areas which were originally authentic but which are 'discovered' and exploited for tourism quickly lose their authenticity. Thus, an example of a pseudo-authentic meeting place is an originally authentic meeting place which has been fundamentally altered but where an attempt has been made to retain a superficial image of authenticity. Another example is to be found in museums, which exhibit authentic objects but where the context is a reconstruction. In this case an attempt is made to illustrate authenticity.

Table 8.4 An illustration of the nature of meeting places. The meeting places consist of the total environment of the place, but in the tourism context, the emphasis is on the infrastructure of tourism and tourism products.

	Authentic	**Synthetic**
Stationary	*Provision*: The genuine, untouched aspects of nature and culture	*Provision*: The artificial, for socially created commercial needs
	Example: Facility imbued with an old activity and building culture	*Example*: Theme parks
	Consequence: Place identity	*Consequence*: Placelessness
	Pseudo-authentic products, e.g. museums	
Temporary	*Provision*: The genuine, untouched aspects of nature and culture	*Provision*: The artificial, for socially created commercial needs
	Example: Folk-song festival, amateur ski competition	*Example*: Activities for incentive journeys in Sami culture
	Consequence: Place identity	*Consequence*: Placelessness

This argument leads us to the conclusion that, if the symbol for authenticity is to be strengthened at a destination or in an area affected by tourism, it is important to describe the whole context and development of the community. The authentic consists in presenting a living chain of development where the traditions of the place are shown over time. The opposite implies that a community has become stuck in a static museum condition. If the basic culture and life mode subsists over time in any sense, it should be possible to define this as sustainable development. We shall give some examples of different types of authentic nature and culture tourism products.

One of the first tourism products which, at the same time, has become one of the foremost symbols of Swedish nature tourism and ecotourism is rafting on Klarälven in the province of Värmland. The product idea is simple but ingenious. Somewhat oversimplified, tourists are provided with timber, rope, a tarpaulin and an instructor to assist if the need arises. After that, it is up to the tourist to build a raft and gently float down the river, experiencing nature and stillness. A limit has been set on the number of rafts that may be constructed in one day so that it will remain an experience of the wilderness for the tourist and the activity will not disturb the environment. The limitation may be compared to the restrictions that are applied in a number of American national parks, where the number of visitors per day is limited. The activity may be considered as a nature tourism product in an authentic environment.

An example of a pseudo-authentic nature tourism product is provided by the companies who specialize in putting together activity programmes for companies and organizations, primarily in connection with courses and conferences. These activities may include throwing the boot, casting axes, rifle shooting, and 'put and take' fishing. The common denominator for most of these activities is that nature is used as a backcloth.

An example of an authentic culture tourism product is described by Grahn (1991). Grahn's main point is that in Sweden we seem to be moving towards the impoverishment of rural areas. The probable course of development, according to Grahn, is that small-scale farming will disappear and this will result in fields becoming overgrown with bushes and the population moving away. Grahn maintains that there is a strong link between culture, in the broad sense of the life mode of the country, and tourism. In Grahn's proposal, tourism is intended to protect the existing culture through the creation of a number of culture-preservation tourist areas. These would consist of villages and the surrounding countryside with fields, meadows and woods, and, above all, the areas would be preserved as economically and culturally viable. Some of the examples that he gives involve offering courses to tourists in, for instance, handicraft, popular traditions, flora and fauna, and traditional farming. Further, the tourists would be able to take part in everyday activities in the areas or purchase existing houses and renovate them in a traditional manner, to be used as weekend cottages.

An example of a tourism product in the cultural sphere which may be considered authentic is Mattila Fritid, situated in the Finnskogen district of the municipality of Torsby in northern Värmland in Sweden. In Mattila, the old settlements of the Finnish immigrants are preserved in their original environment. The owner has authentically renovated old buildings; he rents out rooms and cabins, has a restaurant, offers hiking trails and running and ski tracks, and has a traditional Finnish sauna. He sees his facility as part of the development of the district and is also a member of a group concerned with preserving and developing the district as a whole.

Synthetic meeting places are artificial environments which are constructed with the aim of creating and satisfying socially created commercial needs. The environments are primarily developed to entice long-distance visitors or tourists. They have seldom grown organically but have been constructed relatively quickly. These environments are often functionally designed in accordance with the concept of commercial utility. Furthermore, they are often simplified and lack an original local identity. In most cases, synthetic meeting places do not result in sustainable tourism development from an ecological and cultural perspective. There are several reasons for this. First, they are, of course, part of the economic market where the linchpin is commercialism as a lifestyle. This lifestyle hardly represents a beneficial use of resources in a global perspective. Second, the meeting place is intended to generate a considerable amount of travel with its resultant pollution. Third, in most cases, the people who develop synthetic meeting places do not take the original local culture into account. Yet from an economic perspective synthetic meeting places may, if they are successful, be sustainable and provide good job opportunities.

If tourists come to dominate the environment of any of the meeting places mentioned above, this might lead to conflicts with the residents. Simply through their numbers, tourists can dominate a place or control a time–space. The greatest risk of disruptions and conflicts is probably to be found in authentic natural and cultural meeting places. Further, cities are generally better prepared from an economic and social perspective to receive tourists than the countryside. Table 8.5 is an attempt to summarize the discussion in this section. The table indicates, on the one hand, three dimensions of sustainability: geographical and ecological, social and cultural, and economic, and on the other, the authentic or synthetic nature of the tourism product. From a geographical and ecological standpoint, a general adaptation to the environment is required for both authentic and synthetic meeting places. From a social and cultural viewpoint, the authentic places are probably more sustainable than synthetically constructed ones; and finally from an economic perspective, greater product development is required for synthetic products than for authentic ones so that they will continue to attract new and larger groups of visitors.

Table 8.5. Aspects of the preconditions for the sustainability of tourism products.

Tourism product	Sustainability Geographical/ physical/ ecological	Social/ cultural	Economic
Authentic	Requires general adaptation to the environment	+	?
Synthetic	Requires general adaptation to the environment	– (?)	Requires continual product development

SUSTAINABLE DEVELOPMENT AND SUSTAINABLE TOURISM DEVELOPMENT IN VÄRMLAND

Projects and Processes in Sustainable Tourism Development

Sustainable development with an emphasis on the environment has been discussed in the province of Värmland (see Figure 8.7) since the 1980s. Furthermore, practical environmental work is today being carried out by different organizations and at many different levels. A large proportion of the work on sustainable development is coordinated by Miljöaktion Värmland (Environmental Action Värmland).

First, our work on the environment in the province has great breadth. We have ecological farming and bio-fuels. We know a lot about building and living ecologically. We have coordinated waste disposal and we have people who are well-qualified to provide information and education and to form public opinion. We have a number of knowledge-based companies whose business concept is the environment. Second, we are used to co-operating . . . In recent years environmental work in Värmland has expanded at all levels. A growing number of people are becoming involved in an increasing number of projects that have a greater range of application. So words have definitely been translated into deeds. (Miljöaktion Värmland 1994a, p. 1, my translation)

In recent years work on sustainable tourism development has been initiated in Värmland. This work has yet to be coordinated but various groups have started a number of interesting processes, several of which may be seen as pilot projects in the country. In the following I shall mention some ongoing projects and processes.

The first example is the series of seminars that Miljöaktion Värmland has started on 'Hållbar turism i Värmland' (Sustainable Tourism in Värmland). The first meeting was held early in 1995 and the concrete results of the discussions on this occasion were that the majority of the participants, primarily from camping sites in the region, signed an appeal for a sustainable Värmland and that the camping-site owners who took part agreed to implement the process of sorting of waste into fractions and composting at their sites during the year. This seminar was followed by a second before the summer of 1995 entitled 'Forum för ett hållbart Värmland' (Forum for a Sustainable Värmland). This forum included eight working meetings, in one of which was discussed the tourist industry as the spearhead and marketer of a sustainable Värmland. The third seminar in the series was held in the autumn of 1995 and dealt with the question of using solar energy for camping sites etc. and also with the impact of tourism and leisure activities. These seminars can be seen as a stage in the development of a strategy and plan of action for sustainable tourism in Värmland.

The second example concerns the effects of canoe tourism in the Dalsland-Nordmarken (DANO) area, covering the northern part of Dalsland and the western part of Värmland and previously designated as a primary recreation area. An interesting pilot project is in progress there: 'Åtgärder för högutnyttjade turistområden. Kanotturism i DANO-området' (Measures for highly utilized tourist areas. Canoe tourism in the DANO areas).[30] The background to the project is the extensive damage to the natural landscape in certain parts of the area and the idea is to test whether it would be possible to apply the Nature Conservation Act and the Protection of Beaches, Shores and River Banks Act rather than the customs of the public right of access in cases where groups of tourists wished to make use of the natural facilities.

Groups of canoeists (more than six people), for instance, would be directed along fixed routes and to prepared sites with facilities such as fireplaces and toilets for rest and overnight stops. They would pay a small charge for this service. Service and supervision would be carried out by wardens, with a function similar to that of the rangers in some of the national parks in the USA.

The third example is the establishment in Värmland in the early summer of 1996 of an advisory body under the name of 'Värmlands Turistakademi' (The Värmland Tourist Academy) with eighteen members representing various aspects of the tourism industry and other organization involved in tourism issues.[31] The

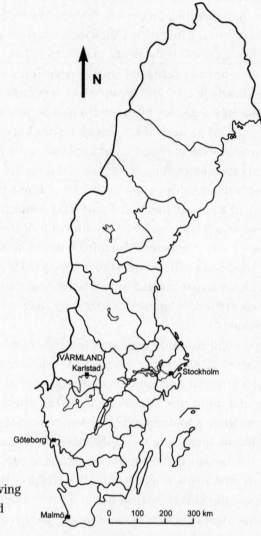

Figure 8.7. Map of Sweden showing county boundaries, Värmland and major cities.

organization has the necessary competence to discuss general issues relating to sustainable tourism development.

It would be interesting to document and evaluate the process of developing more sustainable tourism which has been started in the region, and place it in an international context. Not least important are the international comparisons with countries and regions that have progressed further or worked differently from the manner described here.

The Objective of the Special Study on the Programme 'Ett Hållbart Värmland' (A Sustainable Värmland)

My interest, in this study, is limited to a consideration of the work on sustainable development that is in progress in Värmland (cf. Aronsson 1996, pp. 69–83). The focus is on the programme 'Ett hållbart Värmland' (A Sustainable Värmland), which is being run by the organization Miljöaktion Värmland (Environmental Action Värmland) under the direction of Länsstyrelsen i Värmland (County Administration in Värmland), Landstinget i Värmland (Värmland County Council), Kommunförbundet i Värmland (Värmland Association of Municipalities) and ALMI Företagspartner i Värmland AB (ALMI Enterprise Partners in Värmland AB). The aim is to analyse the actors' most important policy documents, which may be seen as part of the programme. The actors I have studied are Miljöaktion Värmland and its sponsors, mentioned above, and I have analysed their policy documents and some of their studies in the field of sustainable development as well as welfare and environmental issues during 1990–95. More specifically, I deal with the actors' action plans and the systems and structural conditions that they consider need changing if we are to achieve more sustainable development. The presentation begins with a section on method issues in order to provide a context for the specific method I have used: textual analysis.

Method

General comments on methodology

All analyses of data or empirical material in social science are constructions or the results of interpretations (Alvesson and Sköldberg 1994). This statement implies that it is impossible to separate knowledge from the people producing the knowledge irrespective of the method used or the design of the study. This, however, does not mean that we should give up the ambition to conduct serious research but rather that we should point out how important it is for the person producing the knowledge to adopt an attitude towards the research process. There are two basic elements in reflective research, interpretation and reflection, where references to the empirical material are the results of interpretation, and reflection is a kind of interpretation of the interpretation. We are relatively frequently faced in research with a division between quantitative and qualitative methods and they are often claimed to be opposites although this need not be the case. The two methods are in their turn related to different scientific approaches. The aim of a qualitative analysis is to identify the less known but essential features, for instance processes and structures, of something whereas a quantitative analysis is concerned with the frequency and distribution of a feature and the co-variation with other features in the study object in a population (Starrin and Svensson 1994, p. 21). The relation between the quantitative and qualitative methods should be complementary and characterized by mutual dependence. The problem area and aim of a study should be decisive for the choice of method and not vice versa.

A pair of concepts that are related to the quantitative and qualitative methods are the 'context of discovery' and 'context of justification'. The context of discovery refers to the origin and development of a hypothesis or theory and the context of justification to testing the truth value of a hypothesis or theory. The study of the programme for 'A Sustainable Värmland' has been carried out in line with the 'context of discovery' and with the aid of a so-called qualitative method.

The specific method

When the actual study was carried out, the objective stated above proved to be less balanced than had been planned since most of the documents and probably most of the important ones that had been published by Miljöaktion Värmland and its sponsors during the period indicated came from Länsstyrelsen i Värmland. Thus, three of the documents analysed were published by Länsstyrelsen and one by Landstinget i Värmland, whilst ALMI Företagspartner i Värmland AB and Kommunförbundet i Värmland had no written documents of their own on the field or had not documented the ongoing work. However, ALMI has signed and supports Miljöaktion Värmland's appeal for a sustainable Värmland and Kommunförbundet i Värmland is taking part in the ongoing Agenda 21 work in the municipalities in the province. Finally, two documents elucidating the work of Miljöaktion Värmland were examined.[32]

The following approach was used in the analysis of the texts. The documents in question were thoroughly reviewed to establish an answer to the following question: what is the main message in the text? The intention was to determine as accurately as possible the characteristic features of the documents. The next step was to answer the question: what do the respective texts exclude by emphasizing a certain message? The approach, which may be termed a 'path of discovery', enables us to achieve empirically based theory generation (cf. Glaser and Strauss 1967). A fundamental question that should be considered in a textual analysis is whether the documents examined provide an overall picture and are representative of the actors. The question can be resolved by means of supplementary interviews with representatives of the organizations in question. In the present survey the study was sent to representatives of all the organizations involved for their views.

A Sustainable Värmland

Miljöaktion Värmland

Miljöaktion Värmland describes itself as a platform for cooperation between the four main regional actors mentioned. Its organizational base is thus quite broad.

'Miljöaktion's goal is to achieve sustainable development throughout Värmland. The aim is development that does not consume the resources of nature nor harm mankind or the environment' (Miljöaktion Värmland 1994b, p. 1, my translation). Elsewhere Miljöaktion has expressed its goal as: 'working together to fill the map of Värmland with good activities' (my translation).

Miljöaktion operates by:

- spreading information about good environmental initiatives,
- stimulating and supporting ideas and development projects (the interest groups behind Miljöaktion can also provide financial support for different projects),
- identifying new opportunities for the future,
- monitoring environmental and development work in Värmland (Miljöaktion Värmland, 1994a, p. 10).

Miljöaktion Värmland distributes 6000 copies of a newsletter entitled 'Ett hållbart Värmland!' (A Sustainable Värmland).[33] The group targets consumers, producers and different types of organization. In one of its brochures it mentions at least 60 different companies in the county that have the environment as their business concept (Miljöaktion Värmland 1994b, p. 3). Miljöaktion is responsible for, or supports, several different areas:

- Ecologically grown foodstuffs in the county. Miljöaktion says that ecological farming in the county is three times the average level in Sweden. It has also shown a considerable increase in the region during the 1990s.
- Eco-friendly shopping in Värmland. Miljöaktion provides information for consumers about the environmental impact of products.
- Sorting and recycling of waste. This ongoing work is aimed at achieving improvements in waste disposal among consumers, municipal waste collectors and producers.
- Building and living naturally. For example, there are two so-called eco-villages in Karlstad where the consumption of energy and other resources is minimized.
- Bio-fuel instead of oil. Municipalities in the county and the county council are starting to use wood chips and pellets instead of oil as an energy source in thermal power stations.
- Agenda 21 is still in its infancy. There is a large educational element in the work both in spreading the message from the Rio conference and in formulating and attaining local environmental goals.

A promotion day for a sustainable Värmland was held in Karlstad in March 1994 under the aegis of Miljöaktion. The day attracted a broad cross-section of the population in the form of participants and public, and seemed to have great symbolic value.[34] It proved to be another useful method of working. Finally, it should be said that Miljöaktion itself considered its proclamation to be a regional equivalent of the Rio declaration.

Comments

Miljöaktion Värmland is working successfully as a collective forum for all types of environmental commitment. They are striving to inspire, bring together, help the main actors to help themselves and thereby the whole community. Harmony is a fundamental perspective in their work in contrast, for example, to the environmental organization, Greenpeace, whose actions are often controversial and sometimes designed to produce conflict.[35] Miljöaktion concentrates on implementing environmental measures within companies and organizations, and gaining publicity for these measures.

Thoughts on welfare and the quality of life in Värmland

Länsstyrelsen i Värmland has produced a small-in-format, but large-in-content text entitled *Tankar om välfärd och livskvalitet i Värmland* (Thoughts on Welfare and the Quality of Life in Värmland). Its subtitle is 'A memorandum for cooperation between welfare and regional development' (Länsstyrelsen i Värmland 1994a). The document provides an overall, current perspective on welfare and sustainable development for Värmland. One of its most important aims is to promote discussions that will lead to concrete action for better welfare and a sustainable Värmland. Throughout the document the reader is encouraged to ask questions. The content is clearly visionary. The introduction notes that Värmland is a part of the world and is strongly dependent on the outside world. The message is that our relations with the surrounding world have a major influence on our prospects for internal development. The document deals with several different areas, and also demonstrates what is meant by the concept of welfare. Several key areas and strategic processes are identified:

- Healthy nature and an open landscape. Means of achieving this include the use of renewable raw materials and recycling, where waste disposal and the conservation of energy are of major importance. However, if we are to achieve a more sustainable society, it is first and foremost our lifestyles that have to be changed.
- Social networks and supportive environments. Social welfare entails more than the services that are offered by the market and public institutions. Social networks, solidarity within the family and social involvement are encouraged.

- A wide range of industry and a differentiated labour market. For many centuries industry in Värmland has been based on natural resources. This base must today be supplemented with the service and tourism industries. In this context, the tourism industry is cited as an example where Värmland is well situated to provide a wide assortment of products. Here it is also pointed out that all parts of Värmland have an economic value, i.e. the development of rural areas is of particular interest.
- Knowledge and skills are becoming more important as a productive resource and are increasingly being seen as the cornerstone of sustainable development.
- A creative culture. This can be achieved both through the preservation of local and regional diversity and through broad popular participation in political decision-making and social planning.
- Nearness and accessibility both in the region and in getting to it. However, the transport system has a negative impact on the environment. It is therefore important to encourage transport that uses fewer resources and has less environmental impact, to develop renewable forms of energy and to coordinate transport from an environmental perspective.
- A visible Värmland.

> Marketing products from Värmland can be profitably combined with efforts to market Värmland as a region that is well worth visiting. This is important not just for the tourism industry and for the income that Värmland earns from it but also for strengthening our ties with the outside world and for achieving a better understanding between our culture and that of other countries. (Länsstyrelsen i Värmland 1994a, p. 23, my translation)

Comments

The document links theories on and visions of the total life of society with the concrete reality of life in Värmland in an interesting and valid manner. However, it is difficult to say how representative this perspective is of the different divisions in the authority. The document does suggest that a certain perspective is shared by central sections of the organization. The perspective in the document is clearly based on the idea of harmony. But will it ever be possible to pursue a policy of consensus for all of these more or less controversial matters? The harmony perspective also means that the author does not enter into a discussion of the market system's growth treadmill with new and increasing consumption. Even though production is made more efficient through the adoption of processes that consume less energy, and industries are beginning to respect the ecological balance, the in-built logic of the market probably means that more resources will be used. Is this in line with sustainable development?

A strategy for a regional environment

Länsstyrelsen i Värmland is currently supporting a programme in the county entitled 'Strategi för regional miljö' (A Strategy for a Regional Environment) (Länsstyrelsen i Värmland 1994b). The report on the programme is much more thematically restricted in terms of environmental issues than the previous report. Länsstyrelsen has as its goal a good living environment, by which it means:

- A Värmland that is good to live in. Healthy and prosperous inhabitants.
- Rich and varied natural and cultural landscapes with great biological diversity and a vigorous, open, diverse agriculture.
- Healthy soils, water and forests with dynamic plant and animal life.
- A good balance between urban centres and the countryside with suitable housing environments and infrastructure.
- Long term sustainable development based on the natural ecological balance and the husbanding of finite natural resources. (Länsstyrelsen i Värmland 1994b, p. 5, my translation)

All these goals are more or less directly linked to and are of importance for tourism and leisure activities. On the other hand, there are no explicit statements regarding the conditions for and impact of tourism and leisure in the environment except for a few brief statements. According to the authority, the greatest threats to these goals are:

- The acidification of soil and water, the main cause of which is airborne pollutants, mainly sulphur and nitrogen. It is estimated that 80% to 90% of sulphur and nitrogen emissions emanate from outside Sweden.
- The use of soil and water/the impoverishment of biological diversity. The greatest depletion of biological diversity in Värmland is caused, it is assumed, by farmers and forestry companies. The causes are land drainage, rationalization in both farming and forestry resulting in a less varied landscape, and fewer wetlands. The expansion of society's infrastructure in the form of roads, urban centres and power lines has also contributed to a reduction of biological diversity. Most of the county's waterways have been exploited for generating energy and for transport, which has changed the environment for life forms in ecosystems found in these systems.
- Air pollution and noise in urban areas. The authority sees traffic as the main source of dangerous airborne pollutants and noise in the county. Measures to limit cars are of great importance for improving the environment in urban areas.
- Material flows. The authority gives four reasons for the necessity of reducing material flows in society: that the material itself is dangerous for the environment;

that production of the material is dangerous for the environment or is resource-intensive; that the material is based on dwindling resources; and that energy is required to keep the flow moving.

The following are the goals for the environment which the authority has established for Värmland and which directly concern tourism, leisure and outdoor activities:

- One of the overarching goals is that priority should be given to land for outdoor activities close to population centres.
- A further goal is that everyone should have an opportunity for recreation and outdoor activities in a varied landscape.
- It is important to preserve the natural and cultural values of the cultivable landscape. These values can be seen as major resources for tourism and leisure.
- Under the goals for the future use of water, the document states that pollution must not limit the value of lakes and rivers for fishing, outdoor activities or as water for direct consumption.
- The use of land for roads and buildings has increased so that there is very little wilderness left in the province. The document points out that the goal for forestry is that the nearest forest road should not be more that 400–500 metres away, which means that the landscape will be cut into small sections.

Today, more people are using motorized equipment in their outdoor activities, which leads to a noise problem for those seeking peaceful recreation in nature.

Noise from pleasure traffic in the wilderness should not be accepted. The authority feels that such forms of motor traffic are not covered by the public right of access and it will make efforts to reduce the problem of noise in nature. (Länsstyrelsen i Värmland 1994b, p. 29, my translation)

Finally, the document states that:

The authority will attempt to make it more difficult to abuse the public right of access. This entails, for instance, taking steps to prevent inappropriate forms of commercial exploitation of nature, including training and licensing nature preservation wardens. (*ibid.*, p. 29, my translation)

Comments

In parts of the report it is possible to discern a holistic perspective on the environment. In other parts this perspective is fragmentary and there are even some parts where there is a sectoral division of ideas, which makes it harder to see the holistic perspective. This lack of an overall picture is probably due to the fact that there is no common basis underpinning the formulation of the problem. I may further argue that the report repeatedly mentions the goal of sustainable societal development without ever explicitly defining what is meant by the term. On the other hand, there is an emphasis throughout the report on external geographical/physical and ecological environmental factors, which suggests that it is the material dimensions of sustainable development that are being referred to. It is possible to discern a certain conflict of goals in the report. One example is the incompatibility between the goal of reducing emissions from cars and the positive attitude to leisure activities in forests and on water, which entail increased travel.

Regional social planning for an environmentally adapted transport system

Länsstyrelsen i Värmland describes its project entitled 'Regional samhällsplanering för att uppnå ett miljöanpassat transportsystem' (Regional Social Planning for an Environmentally Adapted Transport System) as a general survey (Länsstyrelsen i Värmland 1995). The conclusions will be used in the ongoing project on communications strategy. The authority makes seven basic points in the report:

- The 'hand' structure of the Värmland road system, with Karlstad the regional centre in the palm of the hand, and the surrounding towns at the tips of fingers, as it were, is good for regional development and continued high living standards in Värmland.
- It is important for the development of the Karlstad region to continue, and this will probably mean more commuting, which will, in its turn, lead to greater demands on the intraregional and interregional transport.
- Planners clearly have limited opportunities for optimizing the transport system in the county. The transport solutions devised by large companies, and national and international decisions, are having an increasingly significant impact.
- Areas which are important in terms of conservation, outdoor pursuits or culture, or which represent a natural resource, should be exposed to as little impact as possible. Expansion of the transport system must be balanced against these interests.
- Planned investments in roads and railways have both positive and negative effects. For example, improved traffic safety is seen as positive, whilst encroachment on natural and cultural environments, the net increase of traffic and thus greater emissions are seen as negative.
- In order to achieve the desired environmental goals, public transport must increase its share of travel. This means that it needs support when transport systems are being planned and that a new travel centre should be established in Karlstad.

- In the long term, energy consumption must be based on renewable sources of energy, which means that much of the fossil fuel must be replaced by bio-fuels. This is necessary in order to husband natural resources and reduce the carbon dioxide emissions.

One possible effect might be that the volume of traffic should expand more slowly and that all forms of transport should use fuel more efficiently. The authority believes that a lot of work remains to be done in making transport in the county more eco-friendly. This applies to the use of land, noise and air pollution. Carbon dioxide emissions and energy problems are the most difficult to solve and this will be a factor in determining the dimensions of transport in the future. Electric-powered railways are the most energy-efficient means of transport for goods and people. The authority acknowledges that the road-based transport of people and goods will remain the most dominant form of transport for a long period. Technical solutions, such as making vehicles more eco-friendly, are therefore deemed important. Signals and incentives in the environmental field from the central authorities are important for regional social planning, in influencing manufacturers and affecting individual values. Länsstyrelsen i Värmland concludes by saying that: 'it will be difficult to reduce the environmental effects of traffic to the required targets. It will lead to a troublesome conflict of goals' (Länsstyrelsen i Värmland 1995, p. 13, my translation).

Comments

As its point of departure, the authority has formulated environmental goals for the outer, physical environment, although it does include demands for good regional planning which are more comprehensive and which touch on more than just the physical environment. It is clear in the report that the authority is fully aware of the conflict of goals. One example is that improved communications and economic development often go hand in hand. There is thus an internal conflict between better economic welfare and deterioration in the environment as a result of an expanding transport system. The thrust of the report is interesting because it does not shirk the dilemmas. The question is how the practical solutions to be presented later in the communications strategy will be formulated. Who will the winners be: the promoters of economic growth or the supporters of reduced mobility for the benefit of the environment? Or will there perhaps be a compromise between these opposing interests?

Landstinget i Värmland's political programme for the environment

The county council begins by emphasizing the international links in its political programme for the environment and the importance of thinking globally on environmental matters, and states that it should contribute by making its own activities eco-friendly (Landstinget i Värmland 1990, p. 5). The programme also stresses the fact that each individual has his or her own responsibility towards the environment. The council's basic strategy for a better environment is to move to new technology and new ways of doing things that will prevent problems arising. The council states that environmental considerations should be the guiding principle when investments are made since it is more profitable to choose an eco-friendly alternative from the start, even if the initial costs are higher. The profitability of this approach becomes even clearer when the reduced costs to society for cleaning up environmental damage and dealing with environment-related disease are counted. The main aim of the environmental programme is to ensure the right conditions for good public health in line with the World Health Organization's recommendations. This can be achieved by:

> changing course and aiming for long term sustainable development with minimal environmental impact and a reduced consumption of energy and raw materials. The environment and natural resources must set the limits for our economic and social activities. (Landstinget i Värmland 1990, p. 5, my translation)

The council lists the environmental issues to which attention has mainly been directed in Värmland. Some of those that primarily concern tourism and leisure activities are:

– the environmental impact on lakes, waterways and fishing,
– air pollution in built-up areas and noise from traffic,
– large-scale changes in the landscape – the spread of bushes and trees across the open landscape,
– the exploitation of local recreational areas in some population centres,
– the threat to major parts of the cultural heritage – buildings and objects – because of acid rain (Landstinget i Värmland 1990, p. 4).

Apart from these points, the council underlines the importance of reducing the consumption of energy in all activities and of reducing the consumption of raw materials. It indicates a number of areas for its work on the environment:

• Education in environmental issues and the ways in which sustainable development can be achieved.
• Purchasing and investment. The council is the largest buyer in the county and can use its influence to demand products that cause minimal damage to the environment and use as few resources as possible during their life-cycle. The council has taken a formal decision only to buy swan-marked products, the swan being the symbol of environmental certification by the Nordic Council.
• Chemicals. The council will limit its purchase of chemicals to those that are known not to harm humans and the environment.

- Water and drainage. It is important to maintain the high quality of drinking water and not allow harmful substances to enter the water supply.
- Waste. We have become used to living in a 'rubbish tip' culture. It is now time to take responsibility and reduce the amount of waste, sort waste into fractions and recycle it. Manufacturers must also be encouraged to make products that can be recycled.
- Energy. We must learn to conserve energy, use it more efficiently and use supplies that are local, renewable and eco-friendly. Some examples are bio-fuels, energy forests, energy crops, wind power, solar energy, hydro-electric power and energy generated from waste.
- The transportation of people and goods is very extensive in society. This results in high energy consumption, air pollution, and injuries and deaths in traffic accidents. Major changes are needed in the transport sector.
- Construction. If we use the right technology when we build, we can conserve energy and raw materials. The life-cycle of buildings must be taken into account, from the start of a building project to the administration of the finished building, when its function may change, and finally to its demolition and the recycling of materials.
- Work environment. Work environment issues should be treated in the same way as other operational and financial issues.
- Environmental medicine is about the effect of the physical environment on health, where certain health risks can be avoided by, for example, building better houses and cleaning up traffic environments.
- Influencing public opinion and providing information will help to educate people in environmental concerns which, in turn, will lead to constructive work to the benefit of the environment.
- Forestry, agriculture and the landscape. The programme states that valuable elements in the natural and cultural landscape of Värmland are under threat. This is a negative trend since forestry and agriculture are also of value in terms of leisure and tourism. Fertile environments for plants and animals, along with culturally valuable landscapes, must be protected.

Comments

The council's political programme for the environment concentrates mainly on the physical environment. The environmental problems that the council identifies in its plan of action correspond closely with the views set forth in 'Strategi för regional miljö' (see above). One difference is that the council has a more unified and holistic approach in its programme. The overall picture provided in the council's description means that, on the one hand, each individual is responsible for the environment and that the council can help by providing information, and, on the other, that the council will improve its own organization and adapt its activities so as to benefit the environment. Thus the perspective and presentation mainly concentrate on the relationship between the individual and the organization.

Reflections on the Attitudes of the Actors to People – Environmental Issues

All of the documents discussed talk about sustainable development without ever explicitly defining it. *Tankar om välfärd och livskvalitet i Värmland* (Länsstyrelsen i Värmland 1994a) probably best represents the theoretical and visionary base of a more sustainable society. However, there is no explicit link with a strategy for action. The opposite applies to the work of Miljöaktion Värmland. Theories on sustainable development are not discussed to any great extent. Instead, they are more concerned with the impact on and cooperation between actors in a concrete reality. 'Strategi för regional miljö' deals in relatively limited terms with the human impact on the environment and certain measures that can be taken to reduce environmental problems. As noted earlier, there is little mention of the organization of society and the producer and consumer systems that create the problems. The suggestions for change that are made are therefore of a technically limited character. No changes to the organization of society are recommended. The county council's political programme for the environment concentrates on the relationship between the individual and the organization. This means that the underlying reasons for consumer behaviour are mainly ignored. As has been mentioned, none of the documents covers all of the aspects of the relationship between people and the environment. However, if one takes an overall view of the documents published by the organizations, it is possible to see both a theory (vision) for moving towards a more sustainable society in the future and links to work of a more concrete, practical nature. The fact that major public actors have documented both vision and application is a great strength for the region. Some of the more general consequences of the arguments in the environmental documents on how to achieve sustainable development are:

- The need to increase the knowledge of the general public and organizations on environmental issues in order to achieve long-term changes in behaviour. This can apply to lifestyles, consumer issues and waste disposal.
- At the same time, controlling demand is a matter of national and international regulations and agreements that can affect long-term sustainable development.
- The need to influence manufacturers to implement processes that consume fewer resources, to increase the recycling of materials and reduce the environmental impact of production and products.

- The necessity of improving vehicles and the transport system through technical developments in the sense of reducing their consumption of resources, e.g. designing them to run on renewable fuels and to be recycled, and reducing their negative impact on the environment, particularly in the form of air pollution, noise and the requirement of land. In the last case, it is the transport system for private cars that is most at fault.

It is probable that work on sustainable development will have to proceed on a broad front, i.e. a combination of measures will be necessary.

Sustainable Tourism Development

Common to all these actors is that tourism and leisure activities are not the central issue in their policy statements. When these activities are considered, it is typical of all the documents that tourism is seen as an opportunity for development or a means of regional development. This attitude implies that tourism and leisure activities are not seen as potential environmental problems and thus the actors do not discuss possible restrictions on them.

The consequences of the arguments in the documents, and the ideas these give rise to about how to achieve geographically, physically and ecologically sustainable tourism development, are that:

- The travel flow caused by tourism and leisure activities must be redirected so that greater use is made of more eco-friendly forms of transport than the car. Private motoring, which is the clearly predominant means of transport for tourism in Värmland, adds to air pollution. An increase in the volume of traffic leads to an increase in the emissions despite catalyst exhaust emission control. The use of the car causes noise problems, in particular in urban areas. Noise is also a problem with other forms of transport such as aircraft and trains.
- Connected natural areas and areas of a wilderness type are often divided by roads, which form barriers in nature and may reduce the tourists' enjoyment of nature. At the same time, accessibility is a major factor in the activities we are discussing, which indicates an internal conflict of interest. In this context there is the problem of motorized vehicles being used for outdoor activities in the countryside.
- Efforts should be made to provide experiences and leisure activities in the local environment, in particular where there is a spatial concentration of people. However, this is not without problems. People who live in places far from larger population centres perhaps gain an income and employment from tourism and efforts to reduce long-distance leisure travel may, thus, result in less sustainable economies for these people. Several of the environmental documents I have

studied deal with the contribution of tourism to the maintenance of a living open landscape and to rural development.

- The argument also concerns the public right of access. If the decisions made by each individual to engage in a certain leisure activity are aggregated, this may have consequences which the original individual choice did not intend.
- Tourism has consequences for sustainable development because of the flows of materials in space that it gives rise to. Permanent residents in a place consume a certain share of resources and products. People's lifestyles and consumer patterns as tourists lead, in many cases, to increased consumption and more waste. However, this may vary with the form of tourism.
- Tourism as a means of cultural exchange may be important in the long term in an increasingly segregated and conflictive society. This presupposes, of course, that tourism itself does not lead to conflicts.

CONCLUDING REMARKS

In this Part on the destination, the perspective on sustainable tourism development has been extended from a consideration of environmental issues to cover other important impacts of tourism. First, I discussed tourism from the standpoint of development strategy and the perspective of production theory. Then I considered the various consequences of tourism for the destination. The socio-economic dimension was illustrated primarily by means of a discussion of tourism's production and consumption processes. Further, I considered the geographical and ecological effects of tourism in some detail by referring, among other things, to a case-study of an island, Koster, where a major conclusion was that, from the standpoint of material consumption and waste disposal, the lifestyle of the tourists was more wasteful of resources than that of the residents. I studied the social and cultural impacts of tourism by analysing people's motives for travelling and the forms of tourism they give rise to, and also by analysing the nature of the tourism products and the tourism environment and the impact they have. In the latter case, special attention was given to authentic and synthetic products. The Part concluded with a presentation of a case-study of regional planning for sustainable development, including tourism, in the province of Värmland. This study illustrated how more sustainable development in the region might be achieved.

PART 5

Conclusions

Sustainable Tourism and
Mobile Leisure Development:
What Lessons Can Be Learnt?

CHAPTER 9

Concluding Reflections

IDEAS FOR AN ACTION MODEL FOR PEOPLE, SOCIETY AND ENVIRONMENTAL ISSUES

The analysis in the study provides a basis and generates ideas for an action model for people, society and environmental issues. The model takes its point of departure in the fact that people's present activities are creating problems in the environment. The reasons for this are to be sought in the current systems of production and consumption (the economic system). These systems are intimately linked with and, in many respects, influence people's lifestyles (the socio-cultural system) (cf. Britton 1991; Karlsson 1994; Krippendorf 1989). Thus, people's collective life patterns create a whole series of environmental problems. Various processes also form part of these systems, some of the more important being globalization and the spread of the culture of consumerism. Furthermore, the time–space structure of society has changed considerably over the last hundred years. Present-day society is functionally divided to a high degree and this leads to high levels of mobility. However, the model should not be seen in deterministic terms; people have the collective ability to change their life situation, e.g. through the consumption of eco-labelled goods. Achieving sustainable development is partly a matter of changing attitudes and providing better information, such as getting people to take active responsibility for the environment by reducing their consumption of energy, buying recyclable products and disposing of their waste better. It is also a matter of steering demand by altering national and international regulations and agreements in favour of long-term sustainable development. A change in the direction of a more sustainable society naturally requires governments and other actors, e.g. industry, environmental movements and the scientific community, to reach agreement on the criteria for sustainability (a partnership). There are several ways in which we may seek to change our present, less sustainable system, one being the use of various types of public control mechanisms (cf. Jungen *et al.* 1993),[36] for instance economic ones such as levying a charge on companies' externalities or concentrating on improving the behaviour of individuals with regard to consumption and waste disposal in order to achieve a more sustainable society. Further, society can make use of legal and administrative control mechanisms such as laws, statutes and regulations controlling the right to exploit resources and deposit waste in the countryside and also alter the rules governing those administrative bodies whose job it is to ensure that regulations are observed. It is also possible to devise better technical solutions such as improvements in exhaust emission control for road traffic or noise barriers. Another method is to use socio-cultural control mechanisms such as ethical attitudes to people's rights with respect to nature. Society can use public opinion to influence the views of the individual and thus the collective on such issues as consumption and waste disposal. The problem may also be tackled from a different angle by underlining the opportunities for non-governmental organizations to rouse public opinion and influence companies and authorities. By purchasing eco-labelled products or through regional agreements on ethical rules and/or the eco-labelling of products, organizations can even help to stimulate the production of more eco-friendly goods and services.

The various examples given here show that there are more or less radical measures for achieving more sustainable development, ranging from the introduction of limited solutions, often of a technical or administrative nature, within the present social organization to changes in our whole way of living and in the organization of society. One conclusion is that sustainable development in the strict sense of the word is virtually impossible to achieve without very radical changes in the present global social order. On the other hand, the study shows that it is possible to obtain a more sustainable society than the one we have today if we coordinate a number of different measures. A fundamental question here is whether a territorially based development strategy is necessary if we are to move in the direction of a more sustainable society (Aronsson 1989; Sandell 1996b). The answer to this question may be seen from at least two different angles. First, it is possible that our highly mobile and functional society can become more sustainable as a result of technical developments. On the other hand, people's mental range perhaps requires a sense of belonging to a place; if this is so, we must advocate a territorial development strategy. Further, there are a number of questions that remain unanswered: those referring to people's attitudes to the changes necessary to achieve more sustainable development.

For instance, is it possible for people to have a sense of improved welfare if mobility is relatively limited, with spatially closer contacts between home, work, service, education and leisure activities? And as regards our present consumer behaviour, how would welfare be perceived in a society with greater self-subsistence and recycling within regionally based economies?

REFLECTIONS ON SUSTAINABLE TOURISM AND MOBILE LEISURE DEVELOPMENT

As a result of the spread of consumerism in the world, links are established between demand and supply regions, structures developed and products created at the tourist destinations. This materialistic point of departure can also be coupled with a cultural one, that the search for the experience of the pristine, the non-modern or the marginal in many cases results in travel over greater and greater distances. Further, tourism may be seen as a temporary migration which contributes to the development of a multicultural society. Tourism is thus in itself a force of change at the same time as it forms part of a large whole and context. Through the context and processes of which tourism forms part, it contributes to the thinning of space and the possible creation of placelessness. The context which has been sketched shows that attention to sustainability issues, including physical aspects of the environment, and cultural change, is crucial for tourism in modern society. As I have mentioned, the market system means that we live in a consumer culture. This is particularly true of all the articles we use during our leisure time. From the standpoint of environmental sustainability it is essential that the ongoing process of producing more eco-friendly goods and increasing recyclability, including good waste disposal, should continue. Furthermore, leisure articles should be sustainable in the sense that they should last for a long time. Many products or components in products that we use during our leisure activities are produced and transported over long distances. From an environmental viewpoint it would be preferable to make greater use of regionally based economies, which would reduce the distance between producer and consumer. At the same time, it is essential for the sake of the environment that we develop new transport systems and reduce emissions in the transport sector. A fundamental point here is whether all forms of tourism are an expression of our highly mobile functional society or whether there are forms which may be utilized in a territorial development strategy. Let me therefore summarize and discuss what is usually meant by the concept of sustainable tourism. The sustainable development of tourism and leisure activities is generally a matter of:

- Having a long time perspective as regards the use of resources, which implies that conditions for life on earth should improve or at least be maintained at a good level.
- Maintaining that development can be implemented if it does not damage the environment and is ecologically sound; this can be achieved if all the aspects of tourism are designed to meet the requirements of recyclability.
- Emphasizing cultural sustainability, e.g. developing a destination so that it retains its distinctive nature in its architecture and cultural heritage.
- Developing tourism and leisure activities which contribute to equality and provide the local community with economic and social welfare. This includes permanent employment, which is particularly important in peripheral areas.
- Ensuring that positive developments in the spirit of the above are not a burden for other people or areas or coming generations.

It is important not to see tourism in isolation but to place it in a social context. Naturally, this is also true of surveys and discussions of sustainable tourism development. Further, all aspects of tourism should be included, e.g. lifestyle, in particular in connection with leisure activities, tourism and leisure travel, and tourism at the destinations with their varying carrying capacity.

There are several dimensions to sustainable tourism development; one concerns the economy, where sustainable development should provide good income opportunities for the local community. This leads us to stress the importance of the local and regional economy. Other dimensions relate to the geographical and ecological environment as well as to the social and cultural one. Sustainable tourism development entails keeping the use of and damage to natural and cultural resources to a minimum; if necessary, 'development profits' should be used to improve run-down resources and environments.

In its turn, the social and cultural dimension covers welfare and distribution. The terms 'preservation' and 'change' often recur in the discussion of sustainable development. If everything is preserved in accordance with tradition, this would lead to value conservatism. It is not necessarily the case that everything that is traditional in a society is good. The paradox for sustainable development is that there must be some change in a place. The question is who is to decide what is a good change. From my standpoint the answer is that the extent and speed of change is best determined by the democratic processes in a society, if they are well developed and efficient. This argument means that people at the local level should have the right to exert considerable democratic influence over the development of tourism, since it is at the local level that the consequences are most in evidence. Even this point of departure is problematic since it may mean that the population in an area is faced with the choice of more jobs from a tourist facility or of preserving the natural environment from the impact of that facility. What choice do they make? It is particularly important in the matter of natural resources and nature conservancy to make an overall assessment. Another argument against this view is that even unrestrained bottom-up development is not without risk as a local elite or people with resources can adapt the power structure to suit their own ends. An alternative point of departure is to find a catalyst in a community, e.g. a competent tourism planner, who can both provide the necessary innovations and new knowledge, and also plan for the preservation of fundamental and 'good' traditions. Forceful local planning and management together with cooperative solutions can be seen at least as a complementary model for local tourism development. In an interesting discussion, Smith and Eadington argue in similar terms with regard to several of the above dimensions:

> There is also the socially destabilizing issue of redistribution of income and wealth that invariably follows rapid economic change. Tourism development creates 'winners' and 'losers' among the local residents, often without a common acceptance as to the equity of such redistribution. Alternatively, many of the 'winners' might be outsiders who are then viewed as exploiters of the native population and rapists of the land. Furthermore, the changes in income and wealth are often viewed in light of the long term depletion of an area's resource base; the ability of such destinations to capitalize fully on their tourist resources in the future may become permanently impaired because of rapid tourism development. Good decision making procedures should take all such externalities and their costs fully in account in planning for tourism development and in the evolution of existing tourism industries. Private market forces by themselves cannot rectify such external costs and often ignore altogether – or treat amorally – the income and wealth redistribution issues. When such situations occur, policy makers should structure government intervention to stimulate more desirable outcomes. Regrettably, such enlightened planning is often not realized in practice. (Smith and Eadington 1992, p. 9)

As they observe, sustainable tourism development entails protecting the resource base but it can also be influenced by planning and the choice of sustainable tourism products, i.e. all forms of tourism production which involve a long-term perspective and which are users and not consumers of resources. A further complement to sustainable tourism development is a combination of appropriate tourism products and selective marketing to various target groups of tourists. As regards tourism products that are appropriate for sustainable tourism development, we must set our hopes primarily on the new specialized forms of nature and culture tourism, however, only on condition that they entail shorter travel distances or utilize other forms of transport than those that predominate today. Long-distance leisure travel is an environmental problem that has been less studied in tourism research. The private car is the clearly dominant form of transport for domestic tourism travel whilst air transport predominates in long-distance foreign travel. Both these forms of transport produce high emission and pollution levels and it would be of value for sustainable development to increase the use, for instance, of the train and cycle for tourism travel at the expense of air travel and the private car. The expansion of the transport infrastructure requires a lot of land and is a major factor in changing the landscape. This is particularly true in tourism development and must be taken into account.

One criticism that can be levelled at an investment in the specialized forms of tourism is that they may well attract only elite tourists to an area. If this is the case, what will happen to the social aspect – 'tourism for all'? In this context an elite tourist is one who stays a long time and spends a lot of money. Another danger in concentrating on a very narrow segment of tourists is that economically the market may be too small. Furthermore, it may mean that tourists are not keen to return. Once the tourist has visited a unique tourist destination, he or she chooses a new one for the next trip. Changing mass tourism and adapting it to both the social and ecological environment is just as important as developing new specialized forms of tourism. The main advantages of specialized tourism are first that it offers relatively authentic experiences or natural landscapes; second that it provides complementary income primarily for rural areas; and third that it allows a certain amount of tourism in areas that are attractive but sensitive. However, in this case, a few tourists can have a major impact just because of the sensitivity of the area (Butler 1992, pp. 44–5). Apart from targeting special market segments in, for instance, nature and culture tourism, the strategy should be to concentrate on increasing the tourists' net expenditure rather than on maximizing the number of tourists. This can be achieved by using planning measures to attempt to reduce the leakage in the economy and to encourage the tourists to stay longer.

Principles of a general and practical nature for sustainable tourism and mobile leisure development are outlined below. Responsibility for implementing the principles lies with various actors. First, tourists (the consumers) have their own responsibility. Second, it is essential that industry (the producers), society's organizations at various levels, non-governmental organizations and knowledge organizations work together towards a common and clearly defined goal of achieving greater sustainability.

- Encourage the tourist to read and learn about the culture, nature and social structure of the destination prior to a journey. This can be achieved by the travel agent arranging study circles and providing comprehensive material.
- Increase the knowledge and formal competence in society with regard to issues in sustainable tourism development, such as product development, planning, management and marketing. The educational system is the main actor here but the cooperation of industry is required for implementation.
- Provide information about the impact on the environment of various forms of transport in connection with tourism and leisure travel and develop a transport system and tourism products which minimize the use of energy, pollution, noise and land use. First of all, there is a need for collaboration between actors such the government authorities (apart from collaboration, control instruments and general community planning may also be required) and industry. Second, it is the responsibility of the consumer to gather information about the environmental impact of the various means of transport and act accordingly.
- Develop recreational opportunities close to places, in particular big cities. This may help to eliminate some of the long-distance and energy-consuming travel from large population centres. There is a contradiction here in that the reduction of tourism to peripheral areas will lead to a deterioration in their economic base and a loss of jobs. The primary requirement for developing these leisure activities is collaboration between municipalities and entrepreneurs.
- In peripheral areas, concentrate on increasing the number of products in 'authentic' and certain types of locally based events. Although this means long-distance journeys, the degree of exploitation will be relatively minor if, from the start, the number of simultaneous visitors is limited. In this case what is primarily required is collaboration between entrepreneurs and local planning authorities.
- If tourism products of the public magnet type are to be developed, locate them mainly in densely populated areas which can cope with a large number of visitors better than peripheral areas. Even in this case, it is primarily a matter of collaboration between industry and local authorities.
- In peripheral areas, integrate tourism both economically and socially into the local community. This can be achieved by slow and relatively small-scale expansion, thereby providing the best opportunity for the establishment of economic networks between tourism and other industries. Further, local labour should be used in the tourist industry or alternatively the labour force that moves into the area should be given the chance to become permanent. To achieve this, discerning planning is required on the part of authorities such as municipalities, county administrations and county labour boards as well as collaboration with local industry.

- Support local initiative and give people the chance to participate in the planning process in connection with tourism development. When planning tourism development, the total picture should be taken into account, i.e. both the whole tourism system and its context of other industries and development measures. This is primarily a matter that should be dealt with in the framework of local community planning. Apart from the local residents, other interested parties or actors such as local industry should participate in the planning process.

In conclusion, it is interesting to speculate on the future of tourism and tourists even though it is impossible to say anything definite about future developments (Karlsson 1998). What we can establish is that in any development process different actors (with differing positions of power) have their own ideas of how tourism generally, or a particular place, can and should be represented and these are, of course, a product of their conception of the world. Which actors advocate the development of tourism in a place and which do not? What symbols do the actors use for tourism – and how do they see tourism in the future? This is one of the dimensions that will affect the development of tourism with respect to sustainability.

I have previously noted that a differentiation of tourism products and experiences, and thus of tourist groups as well, is occurring in late modern Western society. However, it is difficult to gauge the extent of this trend. At the same time, Urry (1990) and Rojek (1998) point out that there are signs which would suggest that we already have, as they term it, a 'post-tourist'. This person adopts a special attitude to the often overcrowded tourist destinations. The post-tourist considers the crowds at the tourist destinations as part of the experience. This is far from the romantic ideal of solitude at the top of a mountain. Furthermore, this tourist accepts the commodified world and does not look for authentic values, knowing that they are not to be found. If the post-tourist in this sense does exist, this would seem to presuppose a reflective lifestyle. Even though new tourism products and journeys providing differentiated experiences are on the increase, the question is whether or not the great majority are still 'modern tourists' who take package holidays or are part of what is termed mass tourism. However, it is quite clear that, apart from structural aspects, lifestyle factors are of great importance for the future development of tourism and not least for its sustainability (cf. Aronsson and Wahlström 1999).

Notes

1. Many articles concerning research on the tourist destination are to be found in journals such as *Annals of Tourism Research*, *Journal of Leisure Research*, *Journal of Sustainable Tourism* and *Leisure Studies*.
2. Statistiska Centralbyrån bases its estimates on a special satellite account for tourism. In the figures given here the term 'tourist' includes both leisure tourists and business travellers, e.g. conference participants who travel some distance from their home, stay away from home overnight or cross a country's borders.
3. Note that the tourism industry has a large proportion of part-time employees because of its seasonal nature. The figures for full-time employees include full-time equivalents.
4. Letter from Torsten Hägerstrand dated 31 May 1993.
5. de Kadt (1992, p. 48) classifies development theory in three schools: the neo-classical, Marxism and structuralism.
6. Other documents that were produced included the 'Rio declaration', which contains 27 principles and forms the framework of the programme for sustainable development by underlining the integration of environment and development issues among other things. Further, the Rio conference also discussed 'The Convention on Biological Variety', 'The Climate Convention' and 'Principles for Silviculture'.
7. Sustainable Tourism, World Conference, Lanzarote, Canary Islands, Spain, 24–29 April 1995. Conference information.
8. This plan of action only existed in outline form during the conference and will not be considered here.
9. Sustainable Tourism, World Conference, Lanzarote, Canary Islands, Spain, 24–29 April 1995, Charter for Sustainable Development, p. 12.
10. Eco-label LIFE. NASC. WEST – Ireland – European – Liaison. Brochure.
11. The audit was based on the Environmental Management System, which in its turn was here based on ISO 9000.
12. Apart from the examples of projects given here, Turistdelegationen was working on a programme for sustainable tourism in Sweden when this study was conducted. It is now published in the report: Turistdelegationen (1998).
13. The tourism and travel database (TDB) is an annual telephone survey of about 24,000 Swedes. The data have been collected since 1986. This database contains various kinds of background factors of a similar type to the ones used here. Thus the database has more up-to-date information than that presented here. The problem is that TDB is run on a commercial basis

and it has not been possible to buy the desired material for this study because the costs were much too high.

14. For a more detailed description of the data, see Rydenstam (1992).

15. So-called homogeneity regions or H-regions are used in the material (SCB 1986). In the material, municipalities are placed in H-regions in accordance with the size of their populations, which means that the regions do not have to be geographically coherent. However, their names in the main indicate their location, thus H1 = Stockholm, H2 = Göteborg and Malmö, H3 = Larger cities, H4 = Southern intermediate areas, H5 = Northern population centres, H6 = Northern rural areas.

16. A complicating factor in the survey is the fact that the respondents have indicated main activity and subsidiary activity. Here it is only the main activities that are indicated. Listening to the radio is a typical activity that is probably indicated as subsidiary.

17. The journals are: *Annals of Tourism Research, Journal of Leisure Research, Journal of Sustainable Tourism* and *Leisure Studies*.

18. The first two forms of accommodation are non-commercial and are estimated values. The third form is an estimated value and lies in the grey area between commercial and non-commercial forms of accommodation.

19. A paper with similar content to chapter 5 has been published by Aronsson and Vilhelmson (1998).

20. As regards the delimitation of the data, see Rydenstam (1992) and Vilhelmson (1994a).

21. In this context lifestyle relates to the activities carried out during leisure time; see Vilhelmson (1994b, p. 28).

22. The material in the time-use study was discussed earlier since the same database is used in this study as in Rydenstam (1992), but the two studies have a somewhat different design.

23. The distribution shows the percentage of those who own, rent or have access to a weekend cottage or not. Yes = owns, rents, has access to a weekend cottage, No = does not own, rent, have access to a weekend cottage.

24. The distribution shows the percentage of households who own or have access to a car and those that do not. Yes = owns or has access to a car, No = does not own or have access to a car.

25. Percentage distribution of number of trips by means of transport/travel used during leisure time for those active locally and at a distance, and both groups together, at weekends (Saturdays and Sundays).

26. Leisure activities at weekends (Saturdays and Sundays) linked with mobility for the groups of those active locally and at a distance, and for both groups together.

27. These interest groups are: Banverket (Swedish Railtrack), Bilindustriföreningen (Association of Motor Vehicle Constructors), Boverket (National Housing Administration), Kommunikationsforskningsberedningen (Communication Research Board), Luftfartsverket (Civil Aviation Administration), Naturvårdsverket, NUTEK (National Board for Industrial and Technical Development), Sjöfartsverket (National Maritime Administration), Statens Institut för Kommunikationsanalys (National Institute for Communication Analysis), Svenska Petroleum Institutet (Swedish Petroleum Institute), and Vägverket (National Road Administration), according to Naturvårdsverket (1996a).

28. Cf. Wärneryd (Wärneryd *et al.* 1995, p. 22) who state that life-cycle analyses of cars show that only about 10 per cent of the energy requirement and environmental impact occurs during the production of the car whilst the remaining 90 per cent relates to the use of the car. This raises two issues from an environmental perspective: that it is interesting to analyse the life-cycles of products and that people's consumer habits and lifestyles are important.

29. The following background data were used in SJ's environmental computer program: Banverket, Datasystem BIS; Kommunikationsforskningsberedningen (KFB), Miljöeffekter av transportmedelsval för godstransporter (Environmental effects of the choice of means of transport for goods), KFB (1994, p. 6); Kungliga Tekniska Högskolan (Royal Institute of Technology), Energiförbrukning och luftföroreningar av svensk eldriven järnvägstrafik (Energy

consumption and air pollution from electrically driven rail traffic), Andersson (1994);
Luftfartsverket, Emissionsfaktorer 1995 (Emission factors 1995), Luftfartsverket koncernstab
teknik miljö (95–09–07); Motortestcenter (Motor Test Centre) Exhaust emission from a 2-stroke
locomotive engine (96–03–04); Naturvårdsverket, Emissionsfaktorer mars 1996 (Emission
factors in March 1996); SAS, Avstånd mellan svenska flygplatser, färdplanerings program
RODOS (Distances between Swedish airports, flight planning programme RODOS), SAS Flight
Support 1995; SIKA, SAMPLAN (1995, p. 13), 95–12–13; SJ, SJ linjeregister och
godstransportplaneringssystem, GTPL (SJ's line register and goods transport planning system,
GTPL), SJF 800, 1 version 3; Sjöfartsverket, Svensk Lots Del A (Swedish Pilots, Part A) (1992)
ISSN 0282–809X, Svensk Lots Del 1 (Swedish Pilots, Part 1) (1991) ISSN 0282–809X, Svensk
kusthandbok del 1–5 (Swedish Coastal Handbook, parts 1–5), (1990–94), ISSN 0283–3603;
Vattenfall (National Power Administration), Energiprojekt SJ/ABB – underlag beträffande
elproduktion (Energy project SJ/ABB – data on the production of electricity), Roland
Johansson Vattenfall Energisystem (94–04–14); Statens väg- och transportforsknings-institut,
Energiförbrukning och för olika transporttyper (Energy consumption and exhaust emissions for
various forms of transport), (718:1993); Vägverket, Vägavstånd i Sverige (Road Distances in
Sweden) (1994) ISBN 91–88250–12–1.

30. 'Measures for highly utilized tourist areas. Canoe tourism in the DANO areas' is a collaborative
project involving the County Administrations in Värmland and Dalsland, the tourist boards in
the two provinces and the local councils in the area; see Axelsson *et al.* (1995).

31. The tasks of Värmlands Turistakademi include:
   • supporting and developing the Värmland tourist industry by creating opinion and
   understanding for investments in and arrangements for tourists, and promoting an
   infrastructure that is favourable to the tourism industry,
   • supervising the ongoing quality improvement in tourism in Värmland by actively supporting
   education and in-service training,
   • communicating with the people of Värmland in order to gain acceptance for tourism as an
   industry,
   • taking part in the more long-term and visionary development of tourism in Värmland, by
   initiating discussions and debates, and by providing the competence for the development of
   ideas, and innovation,
   • the members, through their personal qualifications, will provide support for new tourism
   companies as regards business development, contacts with authorities and involving new
   companies in the collaboration on 'tourist Värmland',
   • appointing the industry's representative to Värmlands Turistråd annually,
   • awarding the annual prize to the person or persons/company who have made a significant
   contribution to the development of the Värmland tourist industry. (Värmlands Turistråd,
   1996)

32. The actors and documents discussed in this section are:
   • Miljöaktion Värmland (1994a), Ett hållbart Värmland! Minnen från upptaktsdagen på
   Scalateatern, Karlstad, fredag 25 mars 1994 (A Sustainable Värmland. Notes from the kick-off
   at Scalateatern, Karlstad, Friday 25 March 1994).
   • Miljöaktion Värmland (1994b), Åt vilket håll går du? (In which direction are you going?)
   • Länsstyrelsen i Värmland (1994a), Tankar om välfärd och livskvalitet i Värmland (Thoughts
   on Welfare and Quality of Life in Värmland).
   • Länsstyrelsen i Värmland (1994b), En god livsmiljö i Värmland (A Good Living Environment
   in Värmland).
   • Länsstyrelsen i Värmland (1995), Regional samhällsplanering för ett miljöanpassat
   transportsystem (Regional Social Planning for an Environmentally Adapted Transport
   System).

- Landstinget i Värmland (1990), Miljöpolitiskt program. Antaget av landstingsmötet den 1 oktober 1990 (Environmental Policy Programme. Adopted by the County Council on 1 October 1990).

33. I made a brief examination of these newsletters as they give an indication of what is actually being done. They reveal that the work Miljöaktion is doing accords well with the description given in its policy document.

34. The day concluded with a proclamation written by Miljöaktion Värmland in which organizations were given the opportunity to sign up for the following:

    . . . we want to be involved in developing Värmland into a successful and sustainable region. Sustainable development in Värmland is characterized by the sustainable use of the resources of nature, sustainable business and a high quality of life. Our organization will contribute to this work by:

    1. Adapting and developing its own activities to minimize both the use of resources and the impact on the environment and to be in harmony with the natural cycle.
    2. Giving employees the knowledge necessary for them to take the environment into consideration in their everyday work.
    3. Participating in development projects and shared activities such as training, meetings, networking and seminars that are part of environmental and development work in Värmland.
    4. Providing information about our own work in order to inspire others and provide a follow-up for sustainable progress in Värmland.
    5. Spreading information about this proclamation to employees, customers and suppliers and encouraging new initiatives for sustainable development within and outside our own activities. (Miljöaktion Värmland 1994a)

35. The difference may be due to the fact that Miljöaktion is funded by the public sector whilst Greenpeace is based on voluntary contributions.

36. Länsstyrelsen i Värmland (1994b, p. 4) notes that the impact of social development on the environment can be influenced by:
    - international conventions and agreements,
    - changes in lifestyles,
    - measures by authorities,
    - development of technology and methods.

References

Alvesson, M. and Sköldberg, K. (1994) *Tolkning och reflektion. Vetenskapsfilosofi och kvalitativ metod.* Lund: Studentlitteratur.

Andersson, L. (1987) Probleminriktning och kärna – krav på (regional) geografi. In *Ymer 1987*, pp. 22–32. Stockholm: Svenska Sällskapet för Antropologi och Geografi.

Andersson, L. (1991) An 'Ideal Model' for Handling Development Situations in Marginal Areas. In Gade, O., Miller Jr., V. P. and Sommers, L. M. (eds) *Planning Issues in Marginal Areas.* Vol. 3, pp. 73–84. Occasional Papers in Geography and Planning. Department of Geography and Planning, Appalachian State University, Boone, North Carolina.

Andersson, M. and Ramqvist, K. (1997) *Semesterresor i förändring – en analys av svenskarnas semesterresor under 1950– och 1990– talet.* Avdelningen för Geografi och Turism. Högskolan i Karlstad.

Åquist, A-C. (1992) *Tidsgeografi i samspel med samhällsteori.* Meddelanden från Lunds Universitets Geografiska Institutioner. Avhandlingar 115. Lund: Lund University Press.

Åquist, A-C. (1994) Tidsgeografin. In Öhman, J. (ed.) *Traditioner i Nordisk kulturgeografi*, pp. 129–135. Uppsala: Nordisk Samhällsgeografisk Tidskrift.

Archer, L. J. (1993) *Aircraft Emissions and the Environment: COx SOx HOx och NOx.* OIES Papers on Energy and the Environment EV 17. Oxford: Oxford Institute for Energy Studies.

Aronsson, L. (1989) *Turism och lokal utveckling. En turism-geografisk studie.* Meddelanden från Göteborgs universitets geografiska institutioner. Serie B. No. 79. Kulturgeografiska institutionen, Handelshögskolan vid Göteborgs universitet.

Aronsson, L. (1993) *Mötet. En studie i Smögen av turisters, fritidsboendes och bofastas användning av tid och rum.* Gruppen för regionalvetenskaplig forskning. Forskningsrapport 1993:1. Högskolan i Karlstad.

Aronsson, L. (1994) Sustainable Tourism Systems: The Example of Sustainable Rural Tourism in Sweden. In *Journal of Sustainable Tourism.* Special Issue on Rural Tourism and Sustainable Rural Development. Vol. 2: 1 & 2, pp. 77–92. Channel View Books.

Aronsson, L. (1996) Sustainable Development – a Possibility? An Actor-Structure Analysis of the 'Sustainable Värmland' Programme in Sweden. In Kobayashi, K. and Kita, H. (eds) *Exploring Sustainability: International Symposium on Future of Small Society in a Dynamic Economy.* Tottori, 25–27 October 1995, pp. 69–83. Regional Planning Research Group, Tottori University. Japan.

REFERENCES

Aronsson, L. (1997) Tourism in Time and Space: An Example from Smögen, Sweden. In Lockhart, D. G. and Drakakis-Smith, D. (eds) *Island Tourism: Trends and Prospects*, pp. 118–36. London and New York: Pinter.

Aronsson, L. and Vilhelmson, B. (1998) Weekend Leisure Activities and Mobility in Sweden: An Aspect of Sustainable Lifestyles. In Andersson, L. and Blom, T. (eds) *Sustainability and Development: On the Future of Small Society in a Dynamic Economy*. Research Report 98:8, pp. 278–89. Social Sciences, Regional Science Research Unit, University of Karlstad.

Aronsson, L. and Wahlström, L. (1999) Vad är Turismgeografi? eller Turisten som populärgeograf! In *Nordisk Samhällsgeografisk Tidskrift*. No. 28, pp. 63–77.

Aubert, V. (1969) *Det skjulte samfunn*. 2:a upplagan. Oslo: Universitetsforlaget.

Axelsson, S., Leander, H., Pettersson, A., Ruus, B. and Svärdsby, P. (1995) *Åtgärder för Högutnyttjade Turistområden Kanotturism i DANO-området*. Karlstad: Länsstyrelsen i Värmland.

Bäck-Wiklund, M. and Lindfors, H. (1974) *Lokalsamhället som livsform – idé och verklighet*. Sociologiska institutionen, Göteborgs universitet.

Bäck-Wiklund, M. and Lindfors, H. (1990) *Landsbygd, livsform och samhällsförändring*. Göteborg: Daidalos.

Baltscheffsky, S. (1992) Riokonferensen: Kraftsamling för framtida miljöarbete. In *WWF EKO*. World Wide Fund for Nature (WWF). No. 3, pp. 6–7.

Bell, D. and Valentine, G. (1997) *Consuming Geographies: We are where we eat*. London: Routledge.

Björnberg, U., Bäck-Wicklund, M., Lindfors, H. and Nilsson, A. (1980) *Livsformer i en region*. Sociologiska institutionen, Göteborgs universitet.

Bjurström, E. (1990–91) *Livsstilsreklam vad är det?* No. 3. Stockholm: Konsumentverket.

Blom, T. (1994) *Symbolens betydelse som turistattraktion för stadsturismen: Med exempel från Bryssel*. Forskningsrapport 94:14. Samhällsvetenskap, Högskolan i Karlstad.

Blomström, M. and Hettne, B. (1981) *Beroende och underutveckling. Den latinamerikanska beroendeskolans bidrag till utvecklingsteorin*. Borås.

Britton, S. (1991) Tourism, Capital and Place: Towards a Critical Geography of Tourism. In *Environment and Planning D: Society and Space*. Vol. 9, pp. 451–78.

Burns, P. M. and Holden, A. (1995) *Tourism, a New Perspective*. London: Prentice Hall.

Butler, R. W. (1980) The Concept of a Tourist Area Cycle of Evolution: Implications for Management of Resources. In *Canadian Geographer*. Vol. 24, No. 1, pp. 5–12.

Butler, R. W. (1992) Alternative Tourism: The Thin Edge of the Wedge. In Smith, V. L. and Eadington, W. R. (eds) *Tourism Alternatives: Potentials and Problems in the Development of Tourism*, pp. 31–46. Chichester: Wiley.

Butler, R. W. and Pearce, D. (eds) (1995) *Change in Tourism: People, Places, Processes*. London: Routledge.

Buttimer, A. (1978) Home, Reach and the Sense of Place. In Aldskogius (ed.) *Regional identitet och förändring i den regionala samverkans samhälle*. Uppsala universitet.

Carlestam, G. and Sollbe, B. (eds) (1991) *Om tidens vidd och tingens ordning: Texter av Torsten Hägerstrand*. Stockholm: Byggforskningsrådet.

Christensen, L. R. and Højrup, T. (eds) (1989) *Livstycker: 12 analyser av livsformer og vilkor*. Ringe: Kulturbøger.

Cohen, E. (1972) Toward a Sociology of International Tourism. In *Social Research*. No. 39, pp. 164–82.

Cohen, E. (1974) Who is a Tourist? In *The Sociological Review*. Vol. 22, No. 4, pp. 527–55.

Commonwealth Department of Tourism (1994) *National Ecotourism Strategy*. Australian Government Publishing Service.

Crang, M. (1998) *Cultural Geography*. London: Routledge.

Cronin, L. (1990) A Strategy for Tourism and Sustainable Developments. In *World Leisure and Recreation*. Vol. 32, No. 3, pp. 12–18.

REFERENCES

Cronin, L. (1995) Quote p. 70 in Hunter, C. J. and Green, H. *Tourism and the Environment. A Sustainable Relationship?* London: Routledge.

Crouch, D. (1994) Home, Escape and Identity: Rural Cultures and Sustainable Tourism. In *Journal of Sustainable Tourism*. Vol. 2, Nos 1, 2, pp. 93–101. Special Issue on Rural Tourism and Sustainable Rural Development. Channel View Books.

Dann, G. (1992) Predisposition Toward Alternative Forms of Tourism Among Tourists Visiting Barbados: Some Preliminary Observations. In Smith, V. L. and Eadington, W. R. (eds) *Tourism Alternatives. Potentials and Problems in the Development of Tourism*, pp. 158–79. Chichester: Wiley.

de Kadt, E. (ed.) (1976) *Tourism. Passport to Development? Perspectives on the Social and Cultural Effects of Tourism in Developing Countries.* Published for the World Bank and Unesco. Oxford: Oxford University Press.

de Kadt. E. (1992) Making the Alternative Sustainable: Lessons from Development for Tourism. In Smith, V. L. and Eadington, W. R. (eds) *Tourism Alternatives. Potentials and Problems in the Development of Tourism*, pp. 47–75. Chichester: Wiley.

de Paauw, K. and Perrels, A. (1994) *The Energy Saving Potential of Holidays: Do We Have to Go Dutch?* Paper at the 34th European Congress of the Regional Science Association from 23 to 26 August, 1994.

Eadington, J. M. and Eadington, M. A. (1986) *Ecology, Recreation and Tourism.* Cambridge: Cambridge University Press.

Eco-label LIFE NASC. WEST – Ireland – European – Liaison. Brochure.

Ellegård, K. (1983) *Människa – produktion. Tidsbilder av ett produktionssystem.* Meddelanden från Göteborgs Universitets Geografiska Institutioner. Serie B. No. 72.

Ellegård, K. (1990) *Tidsgeografiska aspekter på samhällsförändringar.* Occasional Papers 1990:3. Kulturgeografiska institutionen. Handelshögskolan vid Göteborgs universitet.

Ellegård, K. (1991) Tidsgeografi. In Vilhelmson, B. (ed.) *Internationell forskning i kulturgeografi. Nio uppsatser om forskningsläget.* Occasional Papers 1991:10, pp. 101–12. Kulturgeografiska institutionen. Handelshögskolan vid Göteborgs universitet.

Finnish Tourist Board (1993) *Sustainable Tourism: The Challange of the 1990s for Finnish Tourism.* Helsingfors.

Finnish Tourist Board *et al.* (1995) *Towards Sustainable Tourism in Finland. The Results of an Eco Audit Experiment in Ten Tourist Enterprises and Suggestions for Further Measures.* Finnish Tourist Board/YSMEK Management Group. Paino Kolibri Vantaa. Finland.

Flavin, C. (1996) Att avvärja hotet om klimatförändring. In *Tillståndet i världen '96.* (State of the World '96), pp. 32–52. Worldwatch Institute. Naturskyddsföreningen, Naturvårdsverket. Stockholm: Naturskyddsföreningens Förlag AB och Naturvårdsverket Kundtjänst.

Flognfeldt jr, T. (1993) *Areal, steid og reiserute.* Rapport nr 1. Begrepsavklaring og analysemodeller. Skriftserien. No. 78. Oppland Distriktshøgskole. Lillehammer.

Flognfeldt jr, T. and Onshus, T. (1996) *Reiselivsundersøkelsen i Ottadalen sommaren 1995.* Rapport No. 1. Data om de tilreisendes forbruk målt i Ottadalen juni–september 1995. Arbeidsnotat. No. 25. Høgskolen i Lillehammer.

Frändberg, L. (1993) Materialflöden och turism på Koster. In Jungen, B. *et al. Om flödens och biflödens verkningar och biverkningar.* Humanekologiska rapporter. No. 19. Avdelningen för Humanekologi. Göteborgs universitet.

Frändberg, L. (1996) *Tourism as Long Distance Mobility: A Quantitative Analysis of Swedes' Leisure Travel from a Sustainability Perspective.* Licentiate Thesis. Section of Human Ecology. Department of Interdisciplinary Studies of the Human Condition. Göteborg University.

Frändberg, L. (1998) *Distance Matters: An Inquiry into the Relation between Transport and Environmental Sustainability in Tourism.* Thesis. Section of Human Ecology. Department of Interdisciplinary Studies of the Human Condition. Göteborg University. Friedmann, J. and Weaver, C. (1979) *Territory and Function: The Evolution of Regional Planning.* London: Edward Arnold.

REFERENCES

Glaser, B. and Strauss, A. (1967) *The Discovery of Grounded Theory*. Chicago: Aldine Publishing Co.

Grahn, P. (1991) Using Tourism to Protect Existing Culture: A Project in Swedish Lapland. In *Leisure Studies*. 10, pp. 33–47.

Gunn, C. A. (1988) *Tourism Planning*. Second edn. New York: Taylor & Francis.

Hägerhäll, B. (ed.) (1988) *Vår gemensamma framtid. Rapport från världskommisionen för Miljö och Utveckling under ordförandeskap av statsminister Gro Harlem Brundtland*. Stockholm: Bokförlaget Prisma och Tidens förlag.

Hägerstrand, T. (1977) *Culture and Ecology – Four Time-geographic Essays*. Rapporter och notiser. No. 39. Institutionen för kulturgeografi och ekonomisk geografi. Lunds universitet.

Hägerstrand, T. (1984) Escapes from the Cage of Routines. Observations of Human Paths, Projects and Personal Scripts. In Long, J. and Hecock, R. (eds) *Leisure, Tourism and Social Change*, pp. 7–20. Edinburgh: Centre for Leisure Research.

Hägerstrand, T. (1985) *Time-Geography: Focus on the Corporeality of Man, Society, and Environment. The Science and Praxis of Complexity*. Tokyo: United Nations University.

Hägerstrand, T. (1989) Globalt och lokalt. In *Svensk Geografisk Årsbok*. Tema miljö och hållbar utveckling. Lund: Gleerupska universitetsbokhandeln.

Hägerstrand, T. Letter from Torsten Hägerstrand dated 31 May 1993.

Hall, D. (1994) Foreign Tourism under Stress: The Albanian 'Stalinist' Model. In *Annals of Tourism Research*. 11, pp. 539–56.

Hall, M. (1992) Tourism in Antarctica: Activities, Impacts, and Management. In *Journal of Travel Research*. No. 4, pp. 2–9.

Hallin, P. O. (1988) *Tid för omställning – om hushålls anpassningsstrategier vid en förändrad energisituation*. Meddelanden från Lunds Universitets Geografiska Institutioner. Avhandlingar 105. The Royal University of Lund: Lund University Press.

Hallin, P. O. (1991) New Paths for Time-Geography? In *Geografiska Annaler*. 73B (3), pp. 199–207.

Hanneberg, P. (1996) *Ekoturism eller ekoterrorism?* Söderköping: Bra Miljö AB.

Harvey, D. (1989) *The Condition of Postmodernity: An Enquiry into the Orgins of Cultural Change*. Oxford: Basil Blackwell.

Harvey, D. (1996) *Justice, Nature & the Geography of Difference*. Oxford: Basil Blackwell.

Hettne, B. (1982) *Strömfåra och kontrapunkt i västerländsk utvecklingsdebatt*. Bakgrundsrapport 8. Stockholm: Naturresurs- och miljökommittén.

Høivik, T. and Heiberg, T. (1977) *Tourism, Selfreliance and Structural Violence*. Publ. S-14–77. Oslo: International Peace Research Institute. PRIO.

Højrup, T. (1983) *Det glemte folk. Livsformer og centraldirigering*. Hørsholm: Institut for Europæisk folkelivsforskning. Statens byggeforskningsinstitut.

Horn, C., Devlin, P. and Simmons, D. (1995) Mountain-Biking, Social Change and Substitution. In Simpson, C. and Gidlow, B. (eds) *Leisure Connections*. Proceedings of the ANZALS Congress, Christchurch, New Zealand, 17–20 January, pp. 83–9. Department of Parks, Recreation and Tourism. Lincoln University.

Hughes, G. (1998) Tourism and the Semiological Realization of Space. In Ringer, G. (ed.) *Destinations: Cultural Landscapes of Tourism*, pp. 17–32. London: Routledge.

Hunter, C. J. (1995) On the Need to Re-Conceptualise Sustainable Tourism Development. In *Journal of Sustainable Tourism*. Vol. 3. No. 3, pp. 155–65.

Jakobsson, L. and Karlsson, J. C. (1992) *Arbete och kärlek. En vandring i svenska livsformer*. Karlstad: Försvarets forskningsanstalt/Högskolan i Karlstad.

Jansson, B. (1994) *Borta Bra Men Hemma Bäst. Svenskars turistresor i Sverige under sommaren*. GERUM. No. 22. Kulturgeografi. Geografiska institutionen. Umeå universitet.

Jungen, B., Frandberg, C. Magnusson, B. Pavia, H. and Lindgren, P. (1993) *Om födens och biflödens verkningar och biverkningar*. Humanekologiska rapporter. No. 19. Avdelningen för Humanekologi. Göteborgs universitet.

REFERENCES

Kamfjord, G. (1993) *Reiselivsproduktet. En introduksjon til den regionale besøksindustrien.* Lillehammer: Reiselivskompetanse A/S. Mjøs-Bok.

Kane, H. (1996) Övergång till hållbar industri. In *Tillståndet i världen '96.* (State of the world '96), pp. 175–90. Worldwatch Institute. Naturskyddsföreningen, Naturvårdsverket. Stockholm: Naturskyddsföreningens Förlag AB och Naturvårdsverket Kundtjänst.

Karlsson, S.-E. (1994) *Natur och kultur som turistiska produkter. En början till en sociologisk analys.* Forskningsrapport 94:11. Samhällsvetenskap. Högskolan i Karlstad.

Karlsson, S.-E. (1998) *Framtidens turism? – ett möjligt svar på en omöjlig fråga.* Uppsats presenterad vid 7:e Nordiska forskarsymposiet i turism, 3–6 december 1998 i Åre. Forskargruppen Turism & Fritid. Högskolan i Karlstad.

Karlsson, S.-E. and Lönnbring, G. (1998) *Turismentreprenörers och turismföretagares livssammanhang – en begynnande analys.* Uppsats presenterad vid 7:e Nordiska forskarsymposiet i turism, 3–6 december 1998 i Åre. Forskargruppen Turism & Fritid. Högskolan i Karlstad.

Keller, C. P. (1984) Centre-Periphery Tourism Development and Control. In Long, J. and Hecock, R. (eds) *Leisure, Tourism and Social Change,* pp. 77–84. Edinburgh: Centre for Leisure Research.

Kelly, J. R. (1983) *Leisure Identities and Interactions.* Leisure and Recreation Studies 1. London: George Allen & Unwin.

Kohr, M. (1992) Miljökris måste lösas med ekonomisk rättvisa. In *Sveriges Natur,* pp. 2–5. Naturskyddsföreningens tidskrift, extranr.

Kosters, M. J. (1992) Tourism by Train: Its Role in Alternative Tourism. In Smith, V. L. and Eadington, W. R. (eds) *Tourism Alternatives. Potentials and Problems in the Development of Tourism,* pp. 180–93. Chichester: Wiley.

Krantz, L-G. and Vilhelmson, B. (1996) *Förändringar av den dagliga rörligheten i Sverige 1978–1994.* Occasional Papers 1996:2. Department of Human and Economic Geography. Göteborg University.

Krippendorf, J. (1989) *The Holiday Makers. Understanding the Impact of Leisure and Travel.* Oxford: Heinemann Professional Publishing.

Laarman, J. and Perdue, R. (1989) Science Tourism in Costa Rica. In *Annals of Tourism Research.* Vol. 16. No. 2, pp. 205–15.

Landstinget i Värmland (1990) *Miljöpolitiskt program.* Antaget av landstingsmötet den 1 oktober 1990. Karlstad.

Lanfant, M.-F., Allcock, J. B. and Bruner, E. M. (eds) (1995) *International Tourism. Identity and Change.* SAGE Studies in International Sociology 47. London: SAGE Publications Ltd.

Lanfant, M.-F. and Graburn, N. H. H. (1992) International Tourism Reconsidered: The Principle of the Alternative. In Smith, V. L. and Eadington, W. R. (eds) *Tourism Alternatives. Potentials and Problems in the Development of Tourism,* pp. 88–112. Chichester: Wiley.

Länsstyrelsen i Värmland (1994a) *Tankar om välfärd och livskvalitet i Värmland.* (Författare Bertil Lundberg). Karlstad: Länsstyrelsen i Värmland.

Länsstyrelsen i Värmland (1994b) *En god livsmiljö i Värmland.* Del 1–3. Remissupplaga. Rapport 1994:5. Karlstad: Länsstyrelsen i Värmland.

Länsstyrelsen i Värmland (1995) *RES. Regional samhällsplanering för ett miljöanpassat transportsystem.* Rapport 1995:11. Karlstad: Länsstyrelsen i Värmland.

Lea, J. (1988) *Tourism and Development in the Third World.* London & New York: Routledge.

Leimgrüber, W. and Imhof, G. (1998) Remote Alpine Valleys and the Problem of Sustainability. In Andersson, L. and Blom, T. (eds) *Sustainability and Development. On the Future of Small Society in a Dynamic Economy.* Research Report 98:8, pp. 385–96. Social Sciences. Regional Science Research Unit. University of Karlstad.

Lenntorp, B. (1993) De fyra nordiska husen – en empirisk studie av materialflöden i samband med husbyggnation. In *NordREFO* 1993:1, pp. 76–111. Information om regionalpolitik och regionalpolitisk forskning i Norden. Helsingfors: Nordiska institutet för regionalpolitisk forskning.

REFERENCES

Lockhart, D. G. and Drakakis-Smith, D. (eds) *Island Tourism: Trends and Prospects*, pp. 118–36. London: Pinter.

Lowyck, E., Van Langenhove, L. and Bollaert, L. (1992) Typologies of Tourist Roles. In Johnsson, P. and Thomas, B. (eds) *Choice and Demand in Tourism*, pp. 13–32. London: Mansell.

Lury, C. (1996) *Consumer Culture*. Cambridge: Polity Press.

Mabogunje, A. L. (1980) *The Development Process: A Spatial Perspective*. London: Hutchinson.

MacCanell, D. (1989) *The Tourist: A New Theory of the Leisure Class*. Second edn. London: Macmillan.

MacCanell, D. (1992) *Empty Meeting Grounds: The Tourist Papers*. London: Routledge.

Malmberg, T. (1980) *Human Territoriality: Survey of Behavioural Territories in Man with Preliminary Analysis and Discussion of Meaning*. Paris: Mouton.

Massey, D. and Jess, P. (eds) (1995) *A Place in the World? Places, Cultures and Globalization*. 4 – The Shape of the World. Explorations in Human Geography. Oxford: Oxford University Press.

Mathieson, A. and Wall, G. (1982) *Tourism. Economic, Physical and Social Impacts*. Harlow: Longman.

McIntyre. N. (1994) *Nature-based Tourism in Australia: Issues and Challenges*. School of Leisure Studies. Griffith University. Queensland. Australia.

Meadows, D. H., Meadows, D. L., Randers, J. and Behrens III, W. W. (1972) *The Limits to Growth*. New York: Universe Books.

Miljöaktion Värmland. (1994a) *Ett hållbart Värmland! Minnen från upptaktsdagen på Scalateatern, Karlstad fredag 25 mars 1994*. Karlstad: Miljöaktion Värmland c/o Länsstyrelsen i Värmland.

Miljöaktion Värmland (1994b) *Åt vilket håll går du?* Karlstad: Miljöaktion Värmland c/o Länsstyrelsen i Värmland.

Miljödepartementet (1991) *Hur mår Sverige? En rapport om miljösituationen*. Bilaga A till regeringens proposition 1990–91: 90. Stockholm.

Miljödepartementet, Miljövårdsberedningen (1995) *Möte om turismutvecklingen i fjällområdena/Miljövårdsberedningens fjälluppdrag*. Lars-Erik Liljelund. Stockholm.

Miljötidningen (1978) Nummer 1.

Miljövårdsberedningen (1994) *Allemansrätt och hållbar turism. Sammanfattning av rundabordssamtal i mars 1994*. Rapport 1994:9. Stockholm.

Morgan, N. and Pritchard, A. (1998) *Tourism, Promotion and Power: Creating Images, Creating Identities*. Chichester: Wiley.

Müller, H. (1992) *Ecological Product Declaration Rather than 'Green' Symbol Schemes*. In *The Tourist Review*. No. 3.

Murphy, P. E. (1985) *Tourism: A Community Approach*. New York: Methuen.

Næss, A. (1992) Bærekraftig utvikling: En begrepsavklaring. In Dahle, B. (ed.) *Bærekraften for næringsutvikling i Bygdesamfunnet: Holdninger, Kultur, Miljø, Natur*. No. 107. Norges idrettshøgskole.

Nash, D. (1992) Epilogue: A Research Agenda on the Variability of Tourism. In Smith, V. L. and Eadington, W. R. (eds) *Tourism Alternatives: Potentials and Problems in the Development of Tourism*, pp. 216–25. Chichester: Wiley.

Naturvårdsverket (1995a) *Miljötillståndet i Sverige 1995*. Rapport 4509. Stockholm: Naturvårdsverket Förlag.

Naturvårdsverket (1995b) *Allemansrätten och kommersen*. Rapport 4446. Stockholm: Naturvårdsverket Förlag.

Naturvårdsverket (1996a) *Åtgärder för att uppnå ett miljöanpassat transportsystem*. Rapport 4511. Stockholm: Naturvårdsverket Förlag.

Naturvårdsverket (1996b) *Forskning och utveckling för en bättre miljö 1996*. En rapport från tretton svenska finansiärer av miljöforskning. Rapport 4514–8. Stockholm: Naturvårdsverket Förlag.

Ogilvie, F. W. (1933) *The Tourist Movement: An Economic Study*. London: P. S. King and Son Ltd.

REFERENCES

Page, S. (1994) *Transport for Tourism*. London: Routledge.

Pearce, D. (1981) *Tourist Development: Topics in Applied Geography*. London: Longman.

Pearce, D. (1987) *Tourism Today: A Geographical Analysis*. London & New York: Longman Scientific & Technical.

Pearce, D. (1992) Alternative Tourism: Concepts, Classifications, and Questions. In Smith, V. L. and Eadington, W. R. (eds) *Tourism Alternatives: Potentials and Problems in the Development of Tourism*, pp. 15–30. Chichester: Wiley.

Pearce, P. L. (1988) *The Ulysses Factor: Evaluating Visitors in Tourist Settings*. New York: Springer-Verlag.

Pigram, J. J. (1992) Alternative Tourism: Tourism and Sustainable Resource Management. In Smith, V. L. and Eadington, W. R. (eds) *Tourism Alternatives: Potentials and Problems in the Development of Tourism*, pp. 76–87. Chichester: Wiley.

Place, S. (1991) Nature Tourism and Rural Development in Tortuguero. In *Annals of Tourism Research*. Vol. 18, No. 2, pp. 186–201.

Policies of the Goss Government (1993) *Nature Tourism: Building a Stronger Queensland. A Nature Tourism Plan for Queensland*.

Poon, A. (1993) *Tourism, Technology and Competitive Strategies*. Wallingford: CABI.

Relph, E. (1976) *Place and Placelessness*. London: Pion.

Ringer, G. (ed.) (1998) *Destinations: Cultural Landscapes of Tourism*. London: Routledge.

Rojek, C. (1998) Cybertourism and the Phantasmagoria of Place. In Ringer, G. (ed.) *Destinations: Cultural Landscapes of Tourism*, pp. 33–48. London: Routledge.

Rojek, C. and Urry, J. (eds) (1997) *Touring Cultures: Transformations of Travel and Theory*. London: Routledge.

Rossel, P. (1988) Tourism and Cultural Minorities: Double Marginalisation and Survival Strategies. In Rossel, P. (ed.) *Tourism: Manufacturing the Exotic*, pp. 1–20. Document 61. Copenhagen: International Work Group for Indigenous Affairs.

Rydenstam, K. (1992) *I tid och otid. En undersökning om kvinnors och mäns tidsanvändning 1990/1991*. Rapport 79. Levnadsförhållanden. SCB.

Sack, R. (1986) *Human Territoriality: Its Theory and History*. Cambridge Studies in Historical Geography. Cambridge: Cambridge University Press.

Sandell, K. (1995) Ekostrategier, humanekologi och friluftsliv. In *Humanekologi: Meddelande från Nordisk förening för humanekologi*. Vol. 14, No. 3/4, pp. 11–22.

Sandell, K. (1996a) Själens friluftsskog – naturkontakt och miljöperspektiv bland friluftsengagerade i Södra Halland. In *Nordisk Samhällsgeografisk Tidskrift*. No. 22, pp. 99–112.

Sandell, K. (1996b) *Platsidentitet, friluftsliv och miljöperspektiv i det framväxande välfärdssamhället*. Kulturgeografi. Institutionen för Samhällsvetenskap. Högskolan i Örebro och avdelningen för Miljöhistoria. Institutionen för Idéhistoria. Umeå universitet.

SCB (1986) Regionala koder för icke-administrativa områden. *Meddelanden i samordningsfrågor MIS*. 1986:4. Stockholm: Statistiska Centralbyrån.

SCB (1993) *Fritid 1976–1991. Levnadsförhållanden*. Rapport 85. Stockholm: Statistiska Centralbyrån.

Schorr, J. B. (1991) *The Overworked American: The Unexpected Decline in Leisure*. New York: Basic Books.

Selwyn, T. (ed.) (1996) *The Tourist Image: Myth and Myth Making in Tourism*. Chichester: Wiley.

SJ stab Information. *Framgång för tåget. Framsteg för miljön*. Brochure.

Smith, S. L. J. (1989) *Tourism Analysis: A Handbook*. London: Longman Scientific & Technical.

Smith, V. L. (1989) *Hosts and Guests: The Anthropology of Tourism*. Second ed. Philadelphia: University of Pennsylvania Press.

Smith, V. L. and Eadington, W. R. (eds) (1992) *Tourism Alternatives: Potentials and Problems in the Development of Tourism*. Chichester: Wiley.

Squire, S. J. (1998) Rewriting Languages of Geography and Tourism: Cultural Discourses of Destinations, Gender and Tourism History in the Canadian Rockies. In Ringer, G. (ed.) *Destinations: Cultural Landscapes of Tourism*, pp. 80–100. London: Routledge.

Starrin, B., Larsson, G., Dahlgren, L. and Styrborn, S. (1991) *Från upptäckt till presentation. Om kvalitativ metod och teorigenerering på empirisk grund*. Lund: Studentlitteratur.

REFERENCES

Starrin, B. and Svensson P. G. (eds) (1994) *Kvalitativ metod och vetenskapsteori*. Lund: Studentlitteratur.

Stöhr, W. B. and Taylor D. R. (eds) (1981) *Development from Above or Below? The Dialectics of Regional Planning in Developing Countries*. Chichester: Wiley.

Sustainable Tourism, World Conference, Lanzarote, Canary Islands, Spain, 24–29 April 1995. Charter for Sustainable Development.

Sustainable Tourism, World Conference, Lanzarote, Canary Islands, Spain, 24–29 April 1995. Conference information.

Svalastog, S. (ed.) (1985) *Turisme ved kysten: Inpassing av reiseliv i lokale samfunn*. Informasjonsserien. No. 55. Oppland Distriktshøgskole. Lillehammer.

Svalastog, S. (1994) *Lokalisering av reiseliv: Om resursanalyser, den romlige fordelning og lokal innpassing*. 2. utgave/2. opplag. Skriftserien. No. 92. 1994. Høgskolen i Lillehammer.

Svalastog, S. (1996) *Kompendium høsten 1996, ressurs- og produksjonsteori del I, samfunnsmessige konsekvenser og analyser*. Avdelningen for reiseliv og samfunnsutvikling. Høgskolen i Lillehammer.

Svedin, U. (1992) The Challenge of the Societal Dimension to Environmental Issues: A Swedish Research Response. In Svedin, U. and Hägerhäll-Aniansson, B. (eds) *Society and the Environment*. Dordrecht: Kluwer.

Svenska Turistföreningen (STF) (1990) *STF Miljöprogram*. STF publikation 2824.

Svenska Turistföreningen (STF) (1994) *Miljöanpassad turism – ekoturism. Policyprogram för Svenska Turistföreningen*.

Sveriges Nationalatlas (SNA) (1992) *Infrastrukturen. Administration, energi och kommunikationer*. Reinhold Castensson (ed.) Kulturgeografiska institutionen. Stockholms universitet/SNA Förlag/Bokförlaget Bra Böcker.

Sveriges Turistråd (1991) *Turism- rekreationsplanering. Ett exempel från Sotenäs kommun i Bohuslän*. Rapport 1991:3. Stockholm.

Törnqvist, G. (1998) *Renässans för regioner: Om tekniken och den sociala kommunikationens villkor*. Stockholm: SNS Förlag.

Travis, A. S. (1992) *Sustainable Tourism Planning and Development: A Paper for Norway and Sweden*. Avdelningen för Geografi och Turism. Samhällsvetenskapliga institutionen. Högskolan i Karlstad.

Turistdelegationen (1997) *1996 års siffror om svensk turism*. Sammanställda av Turistdelegationens analysgrupp, ett samarbete mellan RTS, TuristRådet och Turistdelegationen. Brochure. Stockholm.

Turistdelegationen (1998) *Hållbar utveckling i svensk turistnäring*. Stockholm.

Urry, J. (1990) *The Tourist Gaze: Leisure and Travel in Contemporary Societies*. London: Sage Publications.

Urry, J. (1995) *Consuming Places*. London: Routledge.

Värmlands Turistråd (1996) *Värmlands Turistakademi*. Östen Högman. Maj 1996. Karlstad.

Veblen, T. B. (1976) *Den arbeidsfrie klasse*. Oslo: Gyldendal.

Vilhelmson, B. (1988) *Befolkningens resvanor i tidsperspektiv. Livscykel- och generationsaspekter perioden 1978–1985*. Choros 1988:1. Forskningsrapporter från Kulturgeografiska institutionen. Handelshögskolan vid Göteborgs universitet.

Vilhelmson, B. (1990) *Vår dagliga rörlighet*. Rapport 1990:16. Stockholm: TFB.

Vilhelmson, B. (1994a) *Inledande analys av Tidsanvändningsundersökningen 1990/91 ur rörlighetsaspekt. Datamaterialet. Rörlighetens omfattning och utveckling*. Occasional Papers 1994:13. Kulturgeografiska Institutionen. Handelshögskolan vid Göteborgs universitet.

Vilhelmson, B. (1994b) Rörlighet: en aspekt på relationen livsstil-miljö. In *Nordisk Samhällsgeografisk Tidskrift*, pp. 27–38. Uppsala.

Wärneryd, O., Hallin, P-O. and Hultman, J. (1995) *Den krypande deponeringskrisen. Om kris och omställning, staden och rörligheten*. Lund: Studentlitteratur.

REFERENCES

Wahlström, L. (1984) *Geografiutveckling och geografisk utveckling. Som om platser betydde något.* Series B. No. 76. 1984. Kulturgeografiska institutionen. Göteborgs universitet.

Wahlström, L. (1997) *Bilder av platser II. Exempel på tillämpningsområden.* Occasional Papers 1997:7. Kulturgeografiska institutionen. Göteborgs universitet.

Wallsten, P. (1988) *Rekreation i Rogen: Tillämpning av en planeringsmetod för friluftsliv.* Kommit Rapport 1988:2. Universitetet i Trondheim.

Weaver, D. (1991) Alternative to Mass Tourism in Dominica. In *Annals of Tourism Research.* Vol. 18. No. 3, pp. 414–32.

Whitelegg, J. (1993) *Transport for a Sustainable Future: The Case for Europe.* London: Belhaven Press.

Widstrand, S. (1993) Vad är Ekoturism? In Resetidningen *Vagabond*, pp. 40–2. Bilaga. No. 3. Stockholm.

Wilkinson, P. (1989) Strategies for Tourism in Island Microstates. In *Annals of Tourism Research.* Vol. 16. No. 2, pp. 153–77.

Williams, D. R. and Van Patten, S. (1997) Back to the Future? Tourism, Place, and Sustainability. In Andersson, L. and Blom, T. (eds) *Sustainability and Development. On the Future of Small Society in a Dynamic Economy.* Research Report 98:8, pp. 359–69. Social Sciences. Regional Science Research Unit. University of Karlstad.

Williams, S. (1998) *Tourism Geography.* London: Routledge.

World Commission on Culture and Development (1996) *Our Creative Diversity.* President Javier Pérez de Cuéllar. Paris: UNESCO Publishing.

World Tourism Organization (WTO) (1992) *Tourism Trends to the Year 2000 and Beyond.* Research report presented at EXPO Seville, September 1992, by Robert Cleverdon.

World Tourism Organization (WTO) (1994a) *Global Tourism Trends.* Madrid: WTO.

World Tourism Organization (WTO) (1994b) *Tourism in 1993: Highlights.* Madrid: WTO.

World Tourism Organization (WTO) (1995) *Compendium of Tourist Statistics 1989–1993.* Madrid: WTO.

Worldwatch Institute. (1996) *Tillståndet i världen '96.* (State of the World, 1996). Worldwatch Institute. Naturskyddsföreningen, Naturvårdsverket. Stockholm: Naturskyddsföreningens Förlag AB och Naturvårdsverket Kundtjänst.

World Wide Fund for Nature (WWF) (1995) *WWF och turismen. Miljöanpassad turism and Ekoturism.* Solna.

Zimmermann, E. W. (1972) *World Resources and Industries.* Third ed. W. N. Peach. James A. Constantin. New York: Harper and Row Publishers.

Index

Note: Page references followed by (t) or (f) indicate tables and figures, respectively.